T0326293

Primordial Experience

Primordial Experience

AN INTRODUCTION TO
rDZOGS-CHEN MEDITATION

Mañjuśrīmitra

Translated by NAMKHAI NORBU *and* KENNARD LIPMAN
in collaboration with BARRIE SIMMONS

Shambhala
Boulder
2001

SHAMBHALA PUBLICATIONS, INC.
2129 13th Street
Boulder, Colorado 80302
www.shambhala.com

© 1983, 1986 by Namkhai Norbu, Kennard Lipman,
and Barrie Simmons

All rights reserved. No part of this book may be reproduced
in any form or by any means, electronic or mechanical, including
photocopying, recording, or by any information storage and retrieval
system, without permission in writing from the publisher.

Shambhala Publications makes every effort to print on acid-free,
recycled paper.

Shambhala Publications is distributed worldwide by Penguin Random
House, Inc., and its subsidiaries.

LIBRARY OF CONGRESS CATALOGING-IN-PUBLICATION DATA
Mañjuśrīmitra.
Primordial experience.
Translation of: Rdo la gser źun.
r. Rdzogs-chen (Rñin-ma-pa) 2. Yoga (Tantric Buddhism)
I. Lipman, Kennard. II. Norbu, Namkhai. III. Simmons, Barrie.
s. Title. V. Title: Introduction to Dzog-chen meditation.
BQ7662.4.M313   1986   294.3'923   86-11842
ISBN 978-0-87773-372-0 (PBK.)
ISBN 978-1-57062-898-6 (PBK.)

Front cover: The dharmakaya buddhas Kuntuzangpo
and Kuntuzangmo (Samantabhadra and Samantabhadri).

TO OUR TEACHERS

CONTENTS

FOREWORD

THIS TEXT, known as the *rDo la gser zhun*, "Gold Refined from Ore," is a marvelous introduction and systematization of the outlook, meditation, method of implementation, and goal of the *rDzogs chen* ("the state of total completeness") tradition. The material is presented by means of the concepts of Buddhist philosophy; the author, Mañjuśrīmitra, was a famous and learned Indian scholar of his day.

One ought not to think that since the term *rDzogs chen* does not appear in this text, it is not a text of rDzogs chen. *rDzogs chen* is merely a name; the reality it refers to is nothing other than the actual state of things. Moreover, as it is said, one ought to rely on the intent and not merely on the words. In many of the early texts of rDzogs chen, "the state of pure and total presence" (*byang chub kyi sems, bodhicitta*), "the very core of the state of pure and total presence" (*snying po byang chub kyi sems*), and "the primordial ground of being, the very core of the state of pure and total presence" (*ye gzhi snying po byang chub kyi sems*), are all synonyms for *rDzogs chen*. This state also has other names, such as "the great hypersphere" (*thig le chen po*),[1] "the all-inclusive state of the individual" (*bdag nyid chen po*),[2] "spontaneously perfect" (*lhun grub*),[3] and so on. These different names are just so many ways of generating an understanding of reality in the mind of an individual.

Some people, wanting to dispute the authenticity of rDzogs chen, have stated that the term *rDzogs chen* was not found in the early period of Tibetan Buddhism, and that the many texts that contain this term were fabrications by later scholars. However, the term is clearly found in many early texts, such

as the *bSam gtan mig sgron* of gNubs chen Sangs rgyas ye
shes, a direct disciple of Padmasambhava, as well as in the
Kun byed rgyal po, which is the root *tantra* of the *sems sde*
tradition of rDzogs chen.[4] Not only that, but at the British
Museum in London, among the Tun-huang documents from
the early period, I found a text by the great rDzogs chen yogi
of the period, Sangs rgyas sbas pa (Buddhagupta): the *sBas
pa'i rgum chung.* I found there, as well, the *sems sde* text, *Rig
pa'i khu byug*, together with a commentary.[5] This latter work
is also found in the *Kun byed rgyal po* and is there known as
the "Six Vajra Verses" (*rDo rje tshig drug*).[6] The terms
Atiyoga, i.e., "primordial yoga" (*gdod ma'i rnal 'byor*) and
rDzogs chen are clearly found in these texts.

In the system of the rNying ma pa school, there is a ninefold division of spiritual pursuits: the three ordinary pursuits—that of gods and men, of the Śrāvakas and Pratyekabuddhas, and of the bodhisattvas; the three outer *tantras*—
Kriyā, Cārya, and Yoga; and the three inner, unsurpassable
pursuits—Mahāyoga, Anuyoga, and Atiyoga.[7] Among these,
the three ordinary pursuits primarily teach the way of renunciation (*spong lam*); the three outer *tantras* teach primarily the way of purification (*sbyong lam*); and the three inner
tantras primarily the way of transformation (*sgyur lam*).

Now, Ati, or the primordial yoga (i.e., rDzogs chen), is
supreme, the peak of all spiritual pursuits. But although it is
included here among the three inner, unsurpassable *tantras*, it
does not follow that it belongs to the path of transformation.
Why? Atiyoga proceeds from the fact that the very core of the
primordial state of pure and total presence, through the three
facets of its being [the sheer fact of it's being (*ngo bo*), how
this being actually presents itself (*rang bzhin*), and it's ever-
responsive energies (*thugs rje*)],[8] is a spontaneously self-
generating great *mandala*, whose formative (*sku*) and cognitive (*ye shes*) dimensions can neither be added to nor
subtracted from. By understanding that this is how it is, both
that which muddies the stream of awareness and the actions
that stem from it, which are impure, are naturally freed just

where they arise, without there being something to reject and a means of rejection. Since this primordial state of being can never be tainted by the factors that muddy the stream of awareness and the actions that stem from them, this state is completely beyond that which is to be purified as well as a purifying action. Also, since in this condition the striving and acquiring associated with both pure and impure ways of looking at and dealing with the world have completely come to an end, it is beyond something to be transformed and an activity of transformation. Since there is no need to add to this great *maṇḍala* whose formative and cognitive aspects cannot be added to nor subtracted from (nor indeed anything that could be added to it), one uses the terms "spontaneously perfect," "self-generating ever-fresh awareness," "great primordial purity" (*ka dag chen po*), "primordial lordliness" (*gdod ma'i mgon po*), "state of total completeness," and so forth.

As to clearly showing the intent and viewpoint of intrinsic freedom (*rang grol*) that is the core of Atiyoga or rDzogs chen, terms such as "state of pure and total presence," "great hypersphere," "self-generating ever-fresh awareness," "how it actually is," are all suitable and never indicate anything else than the reality of intrinsic freedom. If one is far from what is intended by intrinsic freedom, then even though one uses grandiose terms like *rDzogs chen* or *Atiyoga*, this does not make it the state of total completeness. Therefore, the profundity of what is meant by *rDzogs chen* should be understood according to the "four reliances": rely on the teacher's message, not on his personality; rely on what is meant, not just on the words; rely on ever-fresh awareness, not on judgmental awareness; and rely on what is definitive, not on what is provisional.[9]

In the supreme, comprehensive spiritual pursuit (*Mahāyāna*), a compassionate mind, which is said to possess the very core of openness and compassion, is called "a mind directed towards pure and total presence" (*byang chub sems, bodhicitta*). What this actually refers to is the open dimension of the total field of events and meanings (*chos dbyings stong pa nyid kyi gnas lugs*). Although this cannot be referred to as "this is it," still, it is not a mere nothing, like a hare's horn, but arises as the unceasing creative excitement of this openness and its limitless, beneficent, charismatic activity (*gzhan phan gyi 'phrin las*). For this reason, even at the stage of developing an attitude directed towards pure and total presence (*sems bskyed, cittotpada*) in the Mahāyāna, through exerting oneself to develop the two relative aspects of this attitude, that is, the aspiration towards it and the steady pursuance of it,[10] one will come to realize the ultimate state of pure and total presence, the profound open dimension of being.

Also, as for the relation of rDzogs chen to the Vajrayana, you should know that in the *tantras, āgamas,* and *upadeśas*[11] of rDzogs chen, the actual condition of the stream of awareness of the individual (*shes rgyud*), just as it is, is explained as the very core of the state of pure and total presence. Therefore, you should understand that *tantra (rgyud)* is just another term for rDzogs chen. So, there is not the least difference between the meanings of *rgyud (tantra)* in rDzogs chen and in the *Anuttarayogatantras. rGyud* ultimately refers to total completeness, the state of pure and total presence, primordial being, the unique fact of awareness, and so forth; and these all refer to the primordial condition of the individual's own stream of awareness. Yet, if we go according to the doctrinal stances regarding *rgyud* in rDzogs chen and in the *tantras,* they are very, very different. Why?

The special methods that the *Anuttaratantras* primarily employ make them a path of transformation, while rDzogs chen is to be distinguished from this in being a path of intrinsic freedom. Now, each path possesses a full set of characteristics that enable it to give rise to this profound genuine condition in each individual. Any text called a "tantra" of the *Anuttarayoga* was transmitted originally through a being who had woken up to his or her capacities (*sangs rgyas, buddha*), out of the dimension of the total richness of reality (*sambhogakāya*), which possesses the five attributes (of teacher, message, etc.);[12] it was then depicted in language. The means to actualize what is at the heart of this teaching is to pursue the way of transformation, through having completed the ten concrete aspects of *tantra*, such as deity, *mantra*, *mudrā*, *samāyā*, and so on.[13] Since, on such a path of transformation, the noble palace of unity can only be made a reality through these, *tantra* here is to be understood as having the ten aspects complete.

rDzogs chen, the path of intrinsic freedom, is completely beyond these ten. Here the spontaneously perfect, all-inclusive primordial state of the individual, the indivisibility of a primordial contact with reality and the awareness that goes with it, is the profound state of total completeness, like a great hypersphere. It is this that is called *tantra* and is ultimately, finally, what *tantra* refers to.

The "Three Incisive Precepts" that were the last testimony of the supreme teacher dGa' rab rdo rje[14] are a means to fully grasp just this. They are direct: introduction to one's own state; not being in doubt about this, through gaining certainty; the certainty of liberation through continuing in this way. This is a summary of all rDzogs-chen teachings. A teaching of such ultimately profound import is a transmission directly from a teacher who is in primordial contact with the total field of events and meanings. This is the "direct transmission lineage," which directly transmits the intention of the Awakened Ones.[15] A transmission through a teacher who is in primordial contact with the full richness of reality occurs through signs and symbols. This is the "symbolic transmission lineage."[16] A transmission through speech and language, by a teacher who is a concrete manifestation of primordial contact with reality, is known as the "oral transmission lineage."[17]

These means of transmission are related to the three types of rDzogs chen texts in the following way: 1) The direct transmission is given by an Awakened One in the dimension of the total field of events and meanings, to a pure audience, whose members are themselves either in the dimension of primordial contact with the full richness of reality or who are concrete manifestations of primordial contact with reality. When set down in words, these transmissions are called *tantras*. 2) Then, those in primordial contact with the full richness of reality, such as Vajrasattva and Vajrapāṇi, reveal, without it being a "teaching," the depth of reality as it is through sound, which is the indestructible communicative quality of that dimension, as well as through various symbols that also indicate that dimension. Their audience is a pure one, consisting of concrete manifestations of primordial contact with reality, those committed to pure and total presence, male and female, and those who possess primordial knowledge, male and female.[18] Then such concrete manifestations teach, in either an extensive or concise manner, to an audience of ordinary beings, and such a teaching, given in words, is known as *āgama*. 3) Finally, concrete manifestations of primordial contact with reality, such as dGa' rab rdo rje and Padmasambhava, explain their own experience of the difficult points in these symbolic and oral teachings to those who possess primordial knowledge, such as Mañjuśrīmitra and Vairocana, to the *ḍākinīs*,[19] and to the most fortunate students among ordinary beings. This is called *upadeśa*.

This text, the *rDo la gser zhun*, is such an *upadeśa*, an oral instruction based on the *tantras* and *āgamas*, and it was one of the five earliest texts of rDzogs chen to be translated by Vairocana into Tibetan.[20] From this work one will be able to see clearly the very core of rDzogs chen and the way in which it is superior to the ways of renunciation, purification, and transformation. It was for this reason that gNubs chen Sangs rgyas ye shes quoted it so many times in his definitive work of the early period, the *bSam gtan mig sgron*.[21]

Despite the difficulty and profundity of the *rDo la gser zhun*, Dr. Lipman, who has a good background in Buddhist philosophy, undertook to translate it with me. I myself, since I was a young man, have had the opportunity to study with twelve great masters of rDzogs chen: rTogs ldan rinpoche O rgyan bstan 'dzin (1893–1955); Grub dbang bla ma Kun dga' dpal ldan (1878–1950); mKhyen brtse'i yan srid rinpoche

Chos kyi dbang phyug (1910–1960); gNas rgyab mchog sprul Blo gros rgya mtsho (1902–1952); dBon stod mkhyen rab Chos kyi 'od zer (1901–1960); rDzogs chen mkhan rinpoche lHa dbang rdo rje (1894–); mKhyen sprul rinpoche Chos kyi blo gros (1896–1959); 'Brug sras rinpoche 'Gyur med rdo rje (1895–?); Gangs dkar rinpoche Chos kyi senge (1903–1956); A yu mkha' 'gro rinpoche rDo rje dpal sgron (died 1953); Nyag bla rig 'dzin Byang chub rdo rje (died 1978); and Nyag sras rinpoche 'Gyur med rgyal mtshan (1932–). From them I received the introduction to study (*lung*), empowerments (*dbang*), and explanation (*khrid*) of the tantras, *āgamas*, and *upadeśas* of the three divisions of rDzogs chen. Mr. Barrie Simmons, a psychologist with a great deal of experience and understanding of both Buddhist thought and the rDzogs chen teaching, was a very, very capable helper in trying to arrive at an English translation. Thus, we were able to produce a translation that I hope communicates the real message of this text.

I hope that through this work the rDzogs chen teaching will become more widely known and, when implemented, become a basis for the happiness of living beings.

NAMKHAI NORBU

PREFACE

SINCE THE PROCESS of translating this text was as important as the final product, in this preface I would like to give the reader some idea of it. This will also serve as a statement of the principles behind our translation.

I undertook this translation with Professor Norbu, a specialist in the literature of the early period of Tibetan Buddhism as well as in the rDzogs chen tradition as a whole, at his recommendation as to the importance of this text for this tradition. Soon after having completed an initial translation, I decided to seek out the proverbial "educated layman," in this case, Barrie Simmons, a psychologist with a long-time involvement in these teachings, to help us move in the direction of a language that opened out more onto common English usage. My choice was particularly apt, for Barrie had previously been a student of English and American literature (a fact unknown to me!), especially the school of "plain English" as exemplified by Ezra Pound, Ford Madox Ford, and others.

As mentioned above, what was needed was a language that "opened out onto" common usage; that is, while a translation from Tibetan dealing with a subject like rDzogs chen cannot really be encompassed within common English usage, this does not mean that it must be represented in a kind of Buddhist tribal language.[1] Let me give two examples of what I mean by a "Buddhist tribal language," one from our initial translation, one from a widely circulated translation. (Obviously, Sanskrit or Tibetan words that have not entered our language to some extent come under this heading.) Our initial translation of the first line of Mañjuśrīmitra's text, together with its commentary, read:

> The Sugata, (who has realized) the twofold nonexistence of identity, who has acquired nonconceptual wisdom and the dimension of dharmadhatu. . . .   [1]

> The unerring realization of the twofold nonexistence of an identity to the personality and to all of reality is itself the nonconceptual wisdom of the Sugata. By obtaining this wisdom, one acquires the knowledge that (accompanies) this, that of the dharmadhatu, as well as the dimension that is inseparable [from it].

This translation was full of tribal jargon: *Sugata, twofold nonexistence of identity, wisdom, dharmadhatu.*

Now our translation reads:[2]

> To the Joyful One, (who has fully grasped) that there is nothing that makes both (persons and phenomena) what they are, who has acquired ever-fresh awareness untainted by concepts and primordial contact with the total field of events and meanings;   [1]

> The full grasp, without mistakes, that there is nothing that makes both persons and phenomena what they are, is itself the ever-fresh awareness of the Joyful One, untainted by concepts. Obtaining this fresh awareness, one acquires its domain, the total field of events and meanings, as well as the primordial contact inseparable from that domain.

"There is nothing that makes both (persons and phenomena) what they are," translates *bdag med gnyis*, the famous doctrine of *anātman*, usually translated "no-self." "Full grasp" translates *rtogs*, which is the third of a triad of terms indicating a progressive deepening in the understanding of something: *go ba*, intellectual understanding, getting an idea of something so that at least one can begin to explore it; which leads to *nyams*, experiential, firsthand knowledge; which culminates in *rtogs*, thorough comprehension of what

has been experienced, "Now I really know what that is."
"Ever-fresh awareness" translates *ye shes*, the Tibetan translation adding *ye* ("primordial," "since the very beginning") to
the Sanskrit *jñāna* (*shes-pa*). *Ye* does not refer, however, to
some moment long past, but to the fact that an awareness not
conditioned by inner or outer compulsions is "ever-fresh,"
always "at the beginning," in the "primordial time" before
the world takes hardened forms.

"Primordial contact with the total field of events and meanings" translates *chos sku* (*dharmakāya*). To say that *sku* is the
honorific form of *lus* ("body") that is used, in this case, when
referring to the person of the Buddha, would be correct if the
trikāya referred to the characteristics of a person with the
proper name "Buddha." This is not the case. The texts make
it quite clear that *sku* refers not only to the body, but to the
whole environment that that body gives us access to. For example, in Tantrism, the practice of *sku rdo rje* (*kāyavajra*)
refers to the visualization of a divinity and his or her *man-
ḍala*, or environment. "Primordial contact" is an attempt to
convey this inseparability of individual and environment.[3]
"Total field of events and meanings" renders *chos dbyings*
(*dharmadhātu*); and since *chos* in *chos sku* is short for *chos
dbyings* or *chos nyid* (*dharmatā*), we have translated *chos sku*
thusly. Finally, when *chos* appears by itself, usually in the
plural, *chos rnams*, we render it by "configurations of events
and meanings," where it has the sense of an "element" of
experience as mapped out in the Abhidharma. *Chos* (*dharma*)
is here a term that unites the duality of fact (event) and meaning that we find in our experience; it is the "phenomenon"
that a phenomenological approach to experience, such as the
Abhidharma, deals with. The world is meaningful for us; it
meshes with our sensory and intellectual capacities. A phenomenological approach tries to describe this first without
going into theoretical explanations that look behind the
phenomena.

The main point here is, in our second translation one is

hopefully not blocked from understanding the meaning because of not understanding the *words*; the technical terms are rendered precisely, yet with common words.

The second example of "Buddhist tribal jargon" is from the Trungpa-Fremantle translation of the *Tibetan Book of the Dead*. We use it because it is *better* than most in regard to this problem, for it is a mix of tribal jargon and the very readable, contemporary English characteristic of Trungpa. For example, one finds the following paragraph:[4]

> O son of noble family, this is called the experience of the four wisdoms combined, the passage-way of Vajrasattva. At this time, remember your guru's previous teachings on the showing. If you remember the meaning of the showing you will have faith in your earlier experiences, and so you will recognize them, like the meeting of mother and son or like seeing old friends again. As though cutting off doubt, you will recognize your own projections and enter the pure, changeless path of the dharmata; and through that faith a continuous meditative state will arise, and you will dissolve into the great self-existing form of wisdom and become a sambhogakaya buddha who never falls back.

As indicated above, "wisdom" conveys little of *ye shes*. To paraphrase Ezra Pound, to translate *shes rab (prajñā)* or *ye shes* as "wisdom," as is usually done, is like translating "aardvark," "cat," and "dog" all as "animal" or "quadruped." "Showing," "dharmatā," "self-existing form of wisdom," and "sambhogakāya" are all jargon terms that can be translated in the same clear language that characterizes most of this translation. They just require the same effort of thought that has gone into Trungpa's insightful way of rendering and explaining basic Buddhist concepts (for example, on page 11 of the Commentary, the outmoded translation of *dharmakāya* as "body of truth or law" sticks out like a sore thumb amidst the vivacity of the rest of the language).

We are not merely speaking of stylistic considerations. (I can remember as a student, whenever I raised these issues of translation, a certain professor would reply, "That's a problem of English," as if we all knew perfectly well what *shes rab* or *chos sku* meant and were merely haggling over style.) By working with more or less common words to express something "new" in our language, a link is created between experiences hitherto not represented in our language(s) and the experiences represented by common usage.

Once one has begun to enter into the experiences represented by the Tibetan words, what is needed is for this to "percolate" up through one's "linguistic unconscious," to infiltrate that inexplicable weave of experience and mother tongue that constitutes one's silent ability to spontaneously speak a language, until a new grouping of words "pops up." This is "languaging" as a creative act, what the French philosopher Merleau-Ponty called "authentic" or "first-hand speech—that of the child uttering its first word, of the lover revealing his feelings, of the 'first man who spoke,' or of the writer and philosopher who *reawaken primordial experience anterior to all traditions.*"[5] This is contrasted with "second-order expression," where[6]

> speech is an institution. For all these many commonplace utterances, we possess within ourselves ready-made meanings. They arouse in us only second-order thoughts; those in turn are translated into other words which demand from us no real effort of expression and will demand from our hearers no effort of comprehension. . . . It is, however, quite clear that constituted speech, as it operates in daily life, assumes that the decisive step of expression has been taken. Our view of man will remain superficial so long as we fail to go back to that origin, so long as we fail to find, beneath the chatter of words, the primordial silence, and so long as we do not describe the action which breaks this silence.

In short, the translation of the fundamental terms of Buddhist thought and practice demand authentic, firsthand speech because they point to that "primordial experience anterior to all traditions." This has long been insisted upon by the tradition itself: rely not on the words of a teaching but on

what they refer to (*don*).[7] What the Buddhist teaching refers
to is a series of experiences, the names for which are usually
descriptive, as far as this is possible within the limits of language. Another French philosopher in the phenomenological
tradition, Paul Ricoeur, has said: "To understand [and thus to
translate] a text is to follow its movement from sense to reference, from what it says to what it talks about."[8] This is what
we have tried to do in making our translation.

For example, in our case Barrie Simmons would ask,
"What does 'intrinsic awareness' or 'the twofold nonexistence
of identity,' or any other term in the tribal language of the
Buddhists, really mean", that is, tell it to me in English. These
jargon terms have become like "second-order speech," con-
venient currency. (This is indeed the function of jargon, to
provide a short-hand for experts so they may communicate
among themselves quickly and easily. This is valid but
dangerous, especially here where the referents are experiences
not easy to come by, and not electronic equipment or the
clearly defined postulates of a science.) By being confronted
with the above-mentioned demand, I had to return to my silent, felt knowledge of my mother tongue to arrive at a new
expression. In this process, what we consider to be the two
main obstacles to good translation were at least confronted:
translationese and the dogma of the literal versus the interpretive translation.[9]

We were able to confront the second, more serious problem through an extremely important intermediate step, which
constituted the transition between a translation based on the
second-order speech of jargon and one based on more authentic, creative expression. That is, I searched for characteristic glosses or striking phrases with which the Tibetans either
defined or characteristically employed their terms—in other
words, a semantic study. This provided the needed link to a
spontaneous, natural expression in my mother tongue. Most
translators of Asian texts, who uncritically accept the dogma
of literal versus interpretive translations, object to such a use
of glosses, etc., because they regard them as interpretations

that are not the literal meaning of the word in question. To translate the gloss is not the same as to translate the word itself, it is said.[10] But here it is not a case of purely "literally" translating a gloss instead of the actual term. The gloss, definition, etc., merely provides a means to jog one's linguistic unconscious.

Let me give a more concrete example: Barrie and I were searching for a translation of one of the most important of all terms, *rig pa*. I began my mental search for glosses, etc. and remembered the beautiful words with which Sog bzlog-pa Blo-gros rgyal-mtshan (b. 1552) began his *khrid yig* on the rDzogs-chen *Sems sde*:[11]

'o skol rnams kyi sems zhes bya ba'i rig rig tur tur po 'di/
kun tu bzang po dang dus mnyams du dang po nyid du
byung ba yin kyang/kun tu bzang pos rang du mkhyen pas
grol/rang re sems can rnams kyis ngo ma shes pas 'khor
mtha' med du 'khyams/

which may be translated as,

Although this swift flash of knowing that we call our "mind" arises in that primordial "time" contemporaneous with Samantabhadra, Samantabhadra, by recognizing this (flash) as his (own state) is free, but each sentient being, by not recognizing it, wanders endlessly in samsara.

This passage is an epitome of the rDzogs chen understanding of *rig pa*. It also accords with its traditional usage in the definition of the "mental" as "cognitive and illumining" (*rig gsal*).[12] Thinking thus, I ventured "the flash of knowing that gives awareness its quality." "There you have it," said Simmons, "English at last." What we have here is a very precise, phenomenologically (i.e., experientially) oriented method,[13] miles away from spur of the moment "intuitions."

This issue of first- versus second-order speech is closely related to an interesting problem of translation alluded to above: when does a word cease to be descriptive of its referent and become a mere name, a sign?[14] For example, it is quite clear that a term like *Buddha* is in some cases used like a proper name, i.e., as a part of second-order speech, and in others as a term descriptive of the experience it attempts to name (especially in Tibetan, with its two components, *sangs* and *rgyas*, "awakening" and "expansion"). Or, a term like *sems* (*citta*) is used in both a very vague, general sense, "mind," as a part of second-order speech, as well as in very specific contexts highly charged with descriptive significance (as in the Yogācāra trend of thought discussed below in the second part of the Introduction).[15] The translator must decide when to treat these terms as names and when as descriptions, and there is plenty of room for diverse judgments here. This is only one of the motives for the practice of multiple translations of a single term. Here the translator also should decide clearly whether or not to try to translate the two or three words, for example, that might make up a compound in Tibetan (such as *sangs rgyas*). That is, he must ask himself, would the translation of these elements serve to bring out the precise descriptive sense of the term? This method is unfortunately turned into a bad joke when one merely translates the elements of a compound without also capturing the referent of the whole term: *zung 'grel* "pair-yoked"; *ngan song*, "bad migrations," etc.[16]

This returns us to the first problem, translationese: a translation should not reflect the syntactical structure of the original language unless the translator feels that a particular syntax carries an important semantic component. Translationese does not enrich our language, it insults it. As Merleau-Ponty said, different languages "are so many ways of 'singing the world'. . . several ways for the human body to sing the world's praises and in the last resort to live it. Hence the *full* meaning of a language is never translatable into another."[17] In short, a translation into English should "sing" in English (not Tinglish, for example).

Finally, I would like to add a word on the difficulty of translating the Tibetan language. Each language breaks up the world differently (i.e., according to its semantics; Merleau-

Ponty's reference above to the different ways in which languages sing was a reference primarily to their phonetics and syntactics). The Tibetan language, through its contact with the Buddhist tradition, especially, developed a highly refined set of experientially based distinctions in the realm of the psyche, not easily rendered into English. At the same time, however, the lexicon of Tibetan is rather limited, and many of these important experientially based terms are used over and over again in many different contexts. Thus, the translator must know these contexts very well in order to make sense of such a term. (Many a time the student stares at a Tibetan sentence, knowing each of the words from other contexts but having little idea of what *this* sentence means). The term *khams* is a good example, given its uses in medicine, all levels of the Buddhist teaching, astrology, etc.

This brings us to another closely related difficulty. Tibetan books were not written for public consumption at the library or bookshop. They were more like messages in code to be used by those deeply involved with a given subject matter. Many of these books were written or dictated by masters who were not highly educated or were even illiterate—in such texts the ambiguity of the Tibetan grammar may be exacerbated, and the need to be well acquainted with the subject matter beforehand an absolute must. This all makes the preparation for becoming a translator of Tibetan a long and difficult task.

In the end, it is I, as the "man in the middle" in the production of this translation, who must accept full responsibility for it, as well as for the introduction and footnotes.

It should be noted that a few Sanskrit terms, such as *samsāra* and *nirvāṇa*, are used in this book as part of our language, and hence given without their diacritical marks.

KENNARD LIPMAN
Formia, Italy

A NOTE

Tibetology and Buddhist studies still resist the revolution that Ezra Pound brought, earlier in this century, to the English rendering of foreign texts. Intelligible versions of Tibetan classics can be counted on one hand. Standards of prose in this field are so low that some published and acclaimed translations are incomprehensible to the dedicated reader.[1]

Profundity of the original is no excuse for the translators' failure to communicate. Pound's own treatment of Confucius, even the deeply philosophical *Chung Yung* (*The Unwobbling Pivot*), proves by example what Wittgenstein argued, that whatever can be thought and said can be said clearly. "The proper man fills his words with meaning."

In Tibetan, the tantras of rDzogs chen employ language transparent to an intelligent farmer, for example, though that may not be true for the writings of the schools. This difference is a matter of principle, as Namkhai Norbu Rinpoche, inspiration and guide of the present work, has often emphasized. Desire and inherent capacity to understand, not a sophisticated vocabulary or mastery of logic, are among the prerequisites for grasping this knowledge.

My role in the book you are reading was kibitzing, what Pound might have called instigation: the nagging demand, which he made of poetry, that translation be as well written as prose. My model was his contribution to the erudite Laurence Binyon's version of the *Divine Comedy* and to W.H.D. Rouse's *Odyssey* and *Iliad*.[2] Reading is hard work, and the writer or translator must help, not hinder. Plain words are his means.

Thirty years ago, while very young, I was lucky enough to study and correspond with Mr. Pound, then in the madhouse, and absorb his endlessly repeated urging to go to the root, go—in the case of Chinese—to the radicals. Since I know no Tibetan, applying this principle to the present task meant asking, again and again, that Dr. Lipman explain to me and to himself, as if we were children or Eskimos, just what he was getting at, what the Tibetan word had meant in its earlier incarnation as Sanskrit, what the Sanskrit word meant syllable by syllable, what the etymology of every term might be, what concrete example he could give for every abstract concept. I had learned from Pound that inside conventional usage, or tired idioms, the original metaphor lies like a fly in amber; so we searched for, and sought to liberate, the image or experience within the words. Where possible, our English equivalents have root meanings close to those of the Tibetan terms. Dr. Lipman was very, very patient.

Much of the merit and none of the confusion of this translation is due to Namkhai Norbu Rinpoche. I have had the good fortune, these last years, to accompany him on some of his travels and put into English his flawless teachings of Dzog chen. He speaks in Italian, a language not his own; he presents the heights and depths of thought; yet his message is always precise, and understandable even to the simple and uneducated. Because he is a Buddha,[3] acting from compassion and lovingkindness, he does all the work and spares the listener any struggle to make out his meaning. Despite my willful stupidity and heart of stone, his image and example have entered into me, coloring many attitudes—including expectations of how teaching should be offered.

The late Fritz Perls, an inspiration to me, demanded clear speech, above all from those who study and claim to explain the mind. He would not tolerate bullshit or bluff. Almost alone in his profession, he insisted on and personally assumed the responsibility of delivering his messages, not just emitting them. He cut through jargon. After him, anyone trying to help others is obliged to talk straight.

Martin Bradley, the painter whose canvases translate
Buddhist vision, can also write. His rendering of the Heart
Sutra, a stimulant to our labors, makes no use of Sanskrit
words, however hallowed or high-sounding. Instead of using
Tathāgata or *dharmadhatu*, we tried, like him, to say it in
English.

This note implies or illustrates how we attempted to reveal
Mañjuśrīmitra's text—a classic because it is still news. I have
tried to state our, or my, debts. May all beings become the
perfection that they truly are!

BARRIE SIMMONS

INTRODUCTION

I

The Text and Its Author

NOT much is known about 'Jam dpal bshes gnyen (Mañ-juśrīmitra). Many of his surviving works deal with the *Mañjuśrīnāmasaṃgīti*, a tantric work.[1] As Padma 'Phrin las (1640–1718) said in his account of the lineage masters of the *'Duṣ pa'i mdo*, the principal tantra of the Anuyoga, "Although one doesn't find a biography of this Ācārya in the ancient texts of the *bka' ma*, there is a slight mention of him in the *sNying thig* and the oral transmission lineage, such as the *rDo rje zam pa*."[2] Nearly all accounts of the rDzogs chen tradition center around his meeting with the first master of rDzogs chen, dGa' rab rdo rje.[3] The picture that emerges from these accounts is the following: he was a learned pandita, probably originally from Ceylon, who was resident at a monastic university (Nalanda is mentioned) at the time when dGa' rab rdo rje was first teaching rDzogs chen as a young man. Virtually all accounts mention Mañjuśrīmitra's knowledge of the prophecy of Mañjuśrī that dGa' rab rdo rje would be teaching a method for liberation in this very lifetime at a cemetery in the land of Oddiyana.

The biography by the eighth-century master Vairocana, the *'Dra 'bag chen mo*, gives the following account:

> The proclamation and maintenance of the extraordinary teaching of the self-originating, effortless state of total com-

pleteness (rDzogs-chen) is as follows: at that time (i.e., of dGa' rab rdo rje), an emanation of the Noble Mañjuśrī, he of supreme intelligence, was born as an intelligent boy-child to the Brahmin dPal ldan bde skyong and the Brahmini Mo ku ta na. He was called "sNying po grub pa" and "bDe mchog snying po." He become learned in all aspects of the teaching of cause and effect, a bhikṣu learned in the five sciences.[4] Among the five hundred pandits (of his monastery) he was supreme. At that time, all the pandits heard that the Nirmāṇakāya dGa' rab rdo rje was proclaiming and maintaining the so-called "effortless state of total completeness," a teaching that is beyond cause and effect, the quintessence of the wondrous teaching (of the Buddhas), superior to all teachings of cause and effect. At just that time the Brahmin sNying po grub pa (heard) the prophecy of Mañjuśrī: "In the northwestern land of O rgyan, on the shore of the Dhanakośa lake, in the valley of He chen bdal ba, in the rDo rje gling cave of the great cemetery of gSer gling, there is an emanation of Vajrasattva, called the Nirmāṇakāya dGa' rab rdo rje, (who has obtained) the empowerment of the 'effortless lamp of all the Buddhas.' Since through him Awakening can be effortlessly realized in an instant through the so-called 'Atiyoga,' the quintessence of the wondrous teachings, you should obtain this and make a collection of (the teachings) of the emanation (dGa' rab rdo rje)." The other scholars wanted to debate (dGa' rab rdo rje) in order to refute, as illogical, the claim that there existed a teaching superior to those of cause and effect.[5]

According to the same *'Dra 'bag chen mo*, the teachings of the first eight *yānas* (Śrāvaka, Pratekabuddha, Bodhisattva, Kriyā-tantra, Caryā-tantra, Yoga-tantra, Mahāyoga-tantra, and Anuyoga-tantra)[6] are all on the level of cause and effect. rDzogs chen or Atiyoga-tantra is said to be a teaching beyond cause and effect in that, for example, it teaches a way of "nonaction" (referred to usually as *rtsol med*, "effortless," in the text). That is, it involves none of the activities of "renunciation" of the *sūtras* (the first three *yānas*), or of "purification" of the lower tantras (the next three *yañas*), or of "transformation" of the higher tantras (the next two *yañas*); but rather is a way of "self-liberation" (*rang grol*).[7] Obviously, the promulgation of such a teaching by dGa' rab rdo rje is taken in these accounts as akin to waving a red flag in front of bulls.

The account continues with the journey and meeting of Mañjuśrīmitra and six of his colleagues with dGa' rab rdo rje. Upon meeting him, Mañjuśrīmitra and some of the other scholars are ashamed at their attempt to argue with dGa' rab rdo rje. Mañjuśrīmitra even swears to cut out his own tongue, but dGa' rab rdo rje tells him that such an action will not purify his obscurations, but that this teaching, which goes beyond causality, will.

The account concludes:

> 'Jam dpal bshes gnyen thoroughly understood in a moment through just a symbolic demonstration.[8] Although he understood thoroughly at this time, in order to completely perfect the teaching, (dGa' rab rdo rje) bestowed the empowerment of "complete reign over realization", and having given completely all the tantras and oral instructions, such as the nine *klong* and 20,000 sections,[9] he also gave (sNying po grub pa) the name "Jam dpal bshes gnyen." Then, summing up the meaning of his instructions, dGa' rab rdo rje sang this Brahma-Song: "Our potentiality for experiencing is actually, from the beginning, fully awakened. Since in this potential for experiencing there is no origination or cessation, it is like the sky. If one understands that all existence is the same in being without origination and cessation, and settles, without striving, in that very (state), that is meditation." At that point, Mañjuśrīmitra thoroughly understood the meaning to be understood, and having perfected the very essence of the teaching, spoke his understanding as follows: "I am Mañjuśrīmitra who has obtained the *siddhi* of Yamāntaka.[10] Thoroughly understanding that samsara and nirvana are really equal, ever-flesh awareness that thoroughly comprehends everything, arises." He then composed, as a summary, the *Byang sems rdo la gser zhun*.[11]

This last statement is very significant for our purposes here, i.e., to try to understand the place of our text, the *Byang chub sems bsgom pa*, nicknamed the *rDo la gser zhun* ("Gold Refined from Ore"), in the rDzogs chen tradition. Whatever credence one may lend to these biographical stories as history, this text appears to be written by a learned Indian scholar, employing the conceptions of classical Buddhist philosophy of a fairly late date (post–sixth century A.D.) when Yogācāra and Madhyamaka philosophy had reached a mature state and various syntheses were being formulated. The text is written in a logical style that is characteristic of some other rDzogs chen texts of the early period in Tibet, such as the *Rin po che rtsod pa'i 'khor lo* of Vairocana.[12] Indeed, in the famous history of dPa' bo gtsug lag, the *mKhas pa'i dga' ston*, this text is characterized as presenting the rDzogs chen *Sems sde*, one of the three principal series of rDzogs chen teachings, through "noncontradictory logical means."[13]

※　※　※

Our text, the 1. *Byang chub sems bsgom pa (Cultivating the Primordial State of Pure and Total Presence)*, is to be found in the various editions of the *bsTan 'gyur*, along with a commentary by an unknown author, the *Byang chub sems bsgom pa don bcu gnyis bstan pa*.[14] There is also a very important commentary in the *Vairocana rGyud 'bum, Theg pa gcod pa'i 'khor lo*, probably by Vairocana himself, which analyzes the verses of Mañjuśrīmitra as a kind of *Grub mtha'*, or critique of philosophical systems, in this case from the Śrāvakas on "up" to rDzogs chen.[15] We have also utilized the commentary by the nineteenth-century rNying ma pa scholar 'Jam ngon 'Ju Mi-pham rgya mtsho, the *Byang chub sems bsgom pa rdo la gser zhun gyi mchan 'grel de kho na nyid gsal ba'i sgron me*, in which he refers to the root text as a "quintessential śastra of the rDzogs chen *Sems sde* in general."[16] Mipham has also made use of the commentary in the *bsTan 'gyur*. There is also another recension of the text in the rNying ma rGyud 'bum, entitled *Byang chub sems bsgom pa'i rgyud theg pa snying po*.[17]

According to the *Vairocana rGyud 'bum* and nearly all sub-sequent scholars,[18] the *Byang chub sems bsgom pa* is one of the *rDzogs chen snga 'gyur lnga*, "the five earliest translations of rDzogs-chen." The other four texts are:

2. *Byang chub sems rig pa khu byug* (*NGB*, Thimbu, vol. 1 (Ka), 419; *DG*, no)[19]
3. *Byang chub sems rtsal chen sprugs pa* (*NGB*, Thimbu, vol. 1 (Ka), 423–4; *DG*, cha, 76a–79b)
4. *Byang chub sems khyung chen* (*NGB*, Thimbu, vol. 1 (Ka), 419–423; *DG*, cha, 79b–86b)
5. *Byang chub sems mi nub pa'i rgyal mtshan* (*NGB*, Thimbu, vol. 1 (Ka), 424–430; *DG*, cha, 86b–88b = *rDo rje sems dpa' nam mkha' che*)

From these and other titles it is apparent that the term *byang chub sems* (*bodhicitta*) figured much more prominently than the term *rDzogs chen* in this early period. According to the fourteenth-century scholar of rDzogs chen, Klong chen rab 'byams pa, in addition to these five early translations there are the thirteen "later translations" (*phyi 'gyur*), which together with the above five make up the eighteen "lower" texts of *Sems sde* (*sems smad*).[20] The thirteen are: 6. *rTse mo byung rgyal*, 7. *Nam mkha'i rgyal po*, 8. *Byang chub sems bde ba 'phra bkod*, 9. *rDzogs pa spyi chings*, 10. *bDe ba rab 'byams*, 11. *Byang chub sems tig*, 12. *Srog gi 'khor-lo*, 13. *Thig le drug pa*, 14. *Byang chub sems rdzogs pa spyi gcod*, 15. *Yid bzhin nor bu*, 16. *Kun 'dus rig pa*, 17. *rJe btsun dam pa*, 18. *bsGom pa don grub*. To these must be added, according to Klong chen pa, 19. *Chos thams cad rdzogs pa chen po byang chub kyi sems kun byed rgyal po* (*The Supreme Ordering Principle of the Universe, the State of Total Completeness in which Every-thing Comes to Full Presence*) and *De'i rgyud phyi ma*, 20. *rMad byung rgyal po*, and 21. *mDo bcu*, to make up the twenty-one basic texts of the *Sems sde*.[21]

dPa' bo gtsug lag gives the following classification and brief characterization of the first seventeen or eighteen texts (see below, note 24) as follows:

THE FIVE GREAT TEXTS

2. is the sign of the arrival of the teaching in Tibet
3. is the sign of completeness and perfection
13. demonstrates contemplation in the same way
4. comprehends the outlook and mode of behavior of all approaches (to the teaching)
5. shows the superiority over other approaches

THE FOUR SMALL TEXTS

15. summarizes all philosophical systems
17. eliminates overevaluation of persons and existents
14. distinguishes the faults and positive qualities of higher and lower approaches
16. forms the basis of the three types of discernment[22]

THE FOUR MIDDLE TEXTS

10. teaches depending on advice (*gdams pa*)
12. shows the *sku, gsung,* and *thugs* of the goal[23]
11. teaches according to examples (*dpe*), their meaning (*don*), and their justification (rtags)
7. teaches according to examples, their meaning, and their justification

THE FOUR TEXTS WHICH PERTAIN TO THE GREAT TEXTS

8. distinguishes between definitive and provisional teachings
9. distinguishes between approaches (to the teaching)
1. does not contradict logic
6. demonstrates mode of behavior and commitments[24]

This grouping of seventeen or eighteen texts goes back to the early period. Our text is mentioned as one of the eighteen fundamental treatises of the *Sems sde* in Nyang ral nyi ma'i 'od zer's (1124–1192) history, the *Chos 'byung me tog snying po sbrang rtsi 'i bcud.*[25] In the chapter on rDzogs chen of the *bSam gtan mig sgron* of gNubs chen sangs rgyas ye shes, the *Byang chub sems bsgom pa* is quoted ten times, always in the company of most of the other of these texts.[26] This chapter also includes a long exposition of Mañjuśrīmitra's teaching of *gnyis su med pa'i lta ba* ("viewpoint of nonduality").[27] The list of eighteen, furthermore, correspond to the chapters of a tantra entitled, *Chos thams cad byang chub kyi sems rdzogs pa chen po 'khor ba rtsad nas gcod pa rin po che dang mnyam pa skye ba med pa'i rgyud*, the last of a group of four tantras on the theme of "fundamental alikeness" (*mnyam pa*).[28] Once again, it is quite common among the rDzogs chen tantras for a chapter to become a separate work, or to find condensed and expanded versions of the same work.

At first glance, it is indeed difficult to tell whether the *Byang chub sems bsgom pa* is in fact a rDzogs chen text, if one is looking for characteristic rDzogs chen terminology, such as *ngo bo, rang bzhin, thugs rje, rtsal, rol pa, 'khregs chod, thod rgal, gzhi*, etc. As mentioned above, it is not surprising that the term *rDzogs chen* is absent from a text of this period, although the *man ngag* to the text found in the *Vairocana rGyud 'bum*, attributed to Mañjuśrīmitra and translated below (p. 35), does use the term *rDzogs chen*. This state of affairs accords well with the traditional account of the genesis of the text given above, in that it tells us that Mañjuśrīmitra was someone new to rDzogs chen when he wrote the *Byang chub sems bsgom pa*.

A likely hypothesis is that Mañjuśrīmitra made the subtle, but qualitatively vast step from the conception of *bodhicitta* found in the tantric works with which he had been familiar as a scholar in India, such as the *Mañjuśrīnāmasaṃgīti* and *Guhyasamājatantra*, to the conception of *bodhicitta* in rDzogs chen. In the above-mentioned works, the conception of *bodhicitta* emphasized is that of the "symbolic origin," i.e., the white moon and seed syllable, out of which the maṇḍala emerges and into which it is reabsorbed. The seed syllable is a symbol of the awakened state of the divinity. Chapter Two of the *Guhyasamājatantra*, for example, is devoted to just such an exposition. It should be noted, however, that there are commentaries that interpret the *Mañjuśrīnāmasaṃgīti* from the rDzogs chen perspective by Vimalamitra and dGa'-rab rdo-rje, but no such work by Mañjuśrīmitra.[29] In

his series of works on the practice of the *Mañjuśrīnāmasaṃgīti*, there is one entitled *Byang chub kyi sems bsgom pa'i man
ngag* that deals with the conception of *bodhicitta* to which we
are referring. It states:

> The meditation on *bodhicitta* by the practitioner of the
> (*Mañjuśrī*)*nāmasaṃgīti* is as follows: having mentally
> envisaged whatever one's *yi dam* is, creatively image
> a vast moon-orb in his heart. At the center of that,
> envisage a white *A*, focusing on that to the exclusion
> of discursive thought.[30]

So here *bodhicitta bhāvanā* means the undistracted creative
imaging of the white *A* as the *symbol* of the unborn nature of
the mind of the divinity, which is usually referred to as part of
the "phase of development" (*bskyed rim*).

In our text, however, processes of creative imagination
through symbols are only employed when one has *not* understood the meaning of realizing *bodhicitta* through the method
of rDzogs chen, which is "nonaction" (*bya ba med pa*). Creative imagination is a mental activity. This issue is the subject
matter of the eighth topic into which the commentary in the
baTan gyur is divided, which is called, "Special methods
taught for fully grasping the real meaning" (lines 124–127). It
is in effect, a summary of Tantrism (as presented in the
Mahāyoga):

> Of the twelve topics, the eighth is: what are the special
> methods taught for fully grasping the real meaning by
> means of transmission through a lineage? The answer is:
>> To really get (the meaning) through symbolic
>> means is also "pure and total presence": so has
>> the Teacher proclaimed.
> For example, just as one gestures to give the meaning
> "Come over here" by a symbolic movement of the right
> hand; so by the activity of focusing the mind one can fully
> comprehend, just as it is, what is meant by "nonaction."
> Moreover, since this makes for the realization of pure and
> total presence, the teacher, the Awakened One, has pro-
> claimed, "It is pure and total presence."

> (The symbolic means) are here the foundation for the activation and cultivation of pure and total presence itself.

The "symbolic encounters"[31] and contemplations pointed out next are the basis, or motivating cause, for the activation and cultivation of the absolutely genuine, primordial state of pure and total presence.

> Having made use of the three "symbolic encounters" that are indicative of (facets of the existence of an Awakened One), and made firm the three contemplations,

When one has not arrived at the real sense of "nonaction," (one employs) the contemplation by focusing without thought; the contemplation that is present everywhere, like the sky; and the contemplation of *A, OM*, etc., the "causal" concentration, which are "the three contemplations."[32]

In summary, we may say that the *Byang chub sems bsgom pa* is one of the fundamental texts of the "mind"-series (*Sems sde*, in which *sems* means *byang chub sems, bodhicitta*) of rDzogs chen, which serves as a general introduction to this teaching by logically demonstrating its outlook (*lta ba*), approach to meditation (*bsgom pa*), and mode of behavior (*spyod pa*) in contrast to the other systems of Buddhist thought. It particularly makes use of concepts found in Cittamātra thought, so much so that the two have often been confused. It is to this issue that we now turn.

II

Sems tsam (Cittamātra) and Sems sde

As mentioned above, our text makes great use of some of the basic concepts of the Yogācāra system of thought, which is also often called Cittamātra (sems tsam),[1] referring to the thesis that there are no "objects-in-themselves" with inherent properties, i.e., how things appear, how they present themselves, does not exist outside of our own experiencing. We find this kind of outlook in the Byang chub sems bsgom pa under the discussion of how the deluded perception of our world, which is the source of frustration and suffering, comes about, entitled, "An inquiry into the nature of that which muddies the stream of awareness (kleśa)," and, "An inquiry into the deceptiveness of how things appear."[2] The basic line of reasoning is as follows:

> It is evident that sentient beings perceive erroneously, because they are tormented by frustration and suffering, as in the perceptions of a drunken or drugged person.
> The source of this error lies in the experiencing process of the individual sentient beings, because it is this experiencing process itself that presents itself as both the internal and external aspects of their reality, as in the case of a meditation in which bones appear everywhere.

Lines 39–41 specify how this situation of delusion comes about:

> (One's potentiality for experience) that always and every-
> where tries to grasp experience through thought, is auto-
> matically enfeebled by this grasping.
> Since one's mental clarity, becoming deluded, has come
> under the power of lack of awareness acting as a con-
> ditioning factor,
> The general forms and specific details of experiencing
> themselves appear as if existing in-themselves, according
> to the three phases (of experience discussed below).[3]

The three phases (*lus*) by means of which the experiencing process presents us with a world of objects, correspond
precisely to the three "transformations" (*pariṇāma, gyur*)
spoken of at the beginning of Vasubandhu's summary of
Yogācāra thought, the *Triṃśika* (*Sum cu pa*), "The Thirty
Verses."[4] These three transformations of the experiencing
process indicate how the "fundamental structuring of all
experience" (*ālaya-vijñāna, kun gzhi rnam par shes pa*)
becomes increasingly conditioned and hardened into the
subject-object dichotomy which is at the root of the un-
satisfactoriness of samsara. These three are given in lines
42–45:

> Through the accumulation of the habituating tendencies
> (engendered by) the various aspects of being caught up in
> a situation, when the power of that habituation has
> grown,
> The potential for experience itself appears in a manner simi-
> lar to that of the body and objects, as in the case of (a
> meditation in which) bones appear everywhere.   [42–43]
> The self, which is imagined by thought when it objectifies
> the continuing stream of habituating tendencies, does not
> exist.   [44]
> By the power of being caught up in experiences, the fun-
> damental structuring of all experiencing has been
> obscured and so this subtle (foundation) is not seen.
> From this specific perceptions arise.   [45][5]

Verses 42–43 represent the first transformation, in which the continuity of the fundamental structuring of all experience as a very subtle process of habituation, out of which all further experience can be specified, is described. It is an indistinct awareness of being in a situation.[6] "Habituation" names that process that gives continuity to our experience, i.e., there is (habitually conditioned) experience of the present in the light of the past, which is itself the "projection" of a (habitually conditioned) future. In this Yogācāra system, it should be remembered that the term *potentiality of experience* or *experiencing process (sems, citta)* is equivalent to the "fundamental structure of all experiencing," the so-called eighth stratum of experiencing, the other seven being specifications or "transformations" of this. Thus, verse 44 describes the second transformation, the formation of the seventh stratum, emotionally perturbed ego-centered consciouness (*kliṣṭa-manovijñāna, nyon mongs kyi yid kyi rnam shes*), which takes the eighth, a momentary flow in which the habituating tendencies are "built up" and "discharged," as an enduring entity called one's "self." Thus, the experiencing of "me, myself" is based on the already "anonymously functioning," i.e., prepersonal,[7] fundamental structuring of all experiencing. Based on this, then, distinct ego-centered perceptions, with which we are usually occupied, can develop through the remaining six strata, the five sense perceptions and the thought process (*manovijñāna, yid kyi rnam shes*). This is the third transformation indicated in verse 45. Verse 62 concludes this line of thought succintly: "Nothing exists for ordinary people and Noble Ones apart from the continuum of their own experiencing."[8]

In the West, it should be noted, the issue of idealism versus realism has been presented, especially since Descartes, under the shadow of the body-mind dualism. The body was always represented as part of the objective world, while the mind was subjective and private, composed of sensations and ideas. Philosophers argued over the primacy of the objective and subjective worlds. The attempt was made to represent perception as either physical (objectively determinable as a bodily process) or mental (subjectively determinable as a mental process), or some miraculous mixture of the two.

But Yogācāra philosophy was not presented under the shadow of mind-body dualism. *Citta, sems,* "mind," "experience," means *embodied* experiencing. As verse 60 of our text states, "in the first moment of experience, one's body and all configurations of events and meanings are present."[9] The beings of the six realms experience water differently because their embodied experiencing is different, not because they have different ("purely mental") *ideas* about water. The body is not just objective and publicly observable. Similarly, the mind is not just subjective and private, but has private and public aspects according to the Yogācārins.[10] This latter aspect is basically the "intersubjective" world of culture. Take gesture (including facial expressions), or language, for example. You'll never explain how people can communicate and understand through gestures or language if you try to force everything into publicly observable, objective, physical processes on the one hand, and private, subjective mental processes on the other. The great French phenomenologist, Merleau-Ponty has said:

> ...the spectator does not look about within himself among his closest experiences for the meaning of the gestures which he is witnessing. Faced with an angry or threatening gesture, I have no need, in order to understand it, to recall the feelings which I myself experienced when I used these gestures on my own account. I know very little, from inside, of the mime of anger so that a decisive factor is missing for any association by resemblance or reasoning by analogy, and what is more, I do not see anger or a threatening attitude as a psychic fact hidden behind the gesture, I read anger in it. The gesture *does not make me think* of anger, it is anger itself.[11]

This type of theory comes about because the theorist is trying to explain how an objective, physical event (the gesture) gets translated into a subjective, private understanding of it as "thought." On the other hand, emotional expressions might be explained as "psychic events" communicated through the body from one consciousness to another through "reasoning by analogy." Regarding this, Merleau-Ponty has also pointed out:

> As Scheler so rightly declares, reasoning by analogy presupposes what it is called on to explain. The other consciousness can be deduced only if the emotional expressions of others are compared and identified with mine, and precise correlations recognized between my physical behaviour and my "psychic events." Now the perception of others is anterior to, and the condition of, such observations, the observations do not constitute the perception. A baby of fifteen months opens its mouth if I playfully take one of its fingers between my teeth and pretend to bite it. And yet it has scarcely looked at its face in a glass, and its teeth are not in any case like mine. The fact is that its own mouth and teeth, as it feels them from the inside, are immediately, for it, an apparatus to bite with, and my jaw, as the baby sees it from the outside, is immediately, for it, capable of the same intentions. "Biting" has immediately, for it, an intersubjective significance.[12]

The point is, there is already, from the beginning of its functioning, an aspect of experiencing that is intersubjective and not in need of objectivist or subjectivist explanations. It is rather that experiencing makes possible objectivism and subjectivism.

Vasubandhu's *Triṃśika* mentioned above is also called *Vijñaptimātratāsiddhi*, "A demonstration that there is just experiencing." This primacy of experiencing is demonstrated by first showing that there is nothing objective existing in-itself apart from experiencing (since the objective is more apparent and people more easily preoccupied with it), and then that there is nothing subjective, existing for-itself apart from experiencing. Usually, *Vijñaptimātra* or *Cittamātra* is translated as "Mind-only," and this "only" is taken to mean a refutation of the external world. Vasubandhu, in his commentary to the *Viṃśatikā*, has indeed said that *mātra (tsam)* means a refutation of the "object" *(artha, don)*.[13] But the sub-commentator, Vinitadeva, informs us that *don* refers to both the subjective and objective sides of experiencing—both do not exist apart from experiencing *(rnam par shes pa las ma gtogs pa gzung dang 'dzin pa'i mtshan nyid kyi don)*.[14] So *artha, don* here means existence in- or for-itself, not the external world. Sthiramati also tells us, "The self as well as the configurations of events and meanings with which it deals both have no 'in-itself' status apart from the experiencing process."[15]

It is important to understand the Yogācāra philosophy properly before one can move on to the critiques of it which follow.

At this point it should be noted that our text does not, however, commit the logical fallacy of believing that its analysis of delusion or the deceptiveness of how things appear is itself outside the realm of this deceptiveness (since it began with the thesis that all the experiences of sentient beings are deluded). Two arguments are used at this point. First, can we confirm with certainty that the experiencing process of sentient beings is the *cause* of error and delusion?; or to put it another way, can we confirm with certainty the very origination of error? Verses 68–73 give a resounding "no" for an answer, in classical Mahāyāna fashion: cause and effect, as all other perceptions, exist only as the discriminations of the experiencing process. But why should we not believe that our thesis applies to itself and is thus false? This objection was also raised against Nāgārjuna's seemingly contradictory statement that he made no claims.[16] Our answer is the same as Nāgārjuna's: his statement is merely a response to the claims of others. Our text says that all cause and effect are merely discriminated through the experiencing process, *because* sentient beings believe that cause and effect exist objectively. The statement is merely an antidote. As Mi pham rgya mtsho, the nineteenth-century commentator on the *Byang chub sems bsgom pa*, said very eloquently on this issue:

Since those who have been habituated, since beginningless time, to an obsessive concern with "entities," have no opportunity to give birth to a fresh awareness (*jñāna, ye shes*) that is free from the four extremes (of existence, nonexistence, both, and neither), first it is necessary (for them) to activate discernment (*prajñā, shes rab*), which is a mental event that discerns that all "entities" are just ultimately nonexistent.[17]

The second argument examines the experiencing process itself. What is it? As mentioned above, it is to be understood as the functioning of the *ālaya vijñāna*, the fundamental structuring, which is itself not other than the moment-by-moment process of habituation (*vāsanā*); i.e., if one (the *ālaya*) exists, the other (*vāsanā*) exists; if one does not exist, the other cannot exist. The basic thesis is applied here again: the habituating tencencies are nothing but false discriminations, and the same must go for the fundamental structuring, their "site." Our text concludes (verse 78): "Therefore, experiencing is beyond the limiting conceptions of existence and nonexistence, and is neither a unity nor a plurality."[18]

So far we have encountered nothing here which goes "beyond" Yogācāra and Madhyamaka philosophy. It seems as if we have, following the text, progressed to a point where we are hanging in a void. To put it simply: the Yogācāra has shown us that the experiencing process is the foundation of delusion; the Madhyamaka has ripped even this foundation out from beneath our feet.[19] All this analysis of error and delusion has been an analysis of the sense in which the experiencing process (*citta, sems*) is the foundation of delusion, or not. Now, *bodhicitta* (*byang chub kyi sems*), however, is not the same as *citta* (*sems*). *Bodhicitta*, "being in a state of pure and total presence," is referred to in our text as *sems kyi rang bzhin*, the "actuality or true nature of experience"; *sems kyi chos nyid*, the "ultimate content of experience"; or *rDo rje sems dpa'* (*Vajrasattva*), "being committed to that which is indestructible." It is not explained in our text according to the sutric conception of *bodhicittotpāda* (*byang chub tu sems bskyed*), the "activation of a compassionate attitude," which is the hallmark of the *bodhisattva*, or according to the tantric conception of *bodhicitta* discussed in the last section. The conception here belongs to rDzogs chen, and no one has explained this conception more clearly, as well as its relation to the Yogācāra philosophy of experience, than Klong chen rab 'byams pa. In many places in his writings he discusses the confusion between *sems sde* and *sems tsam*. To put it simply: in the *sems sde* it is said that "how things appear" (*snang ba*), whether it be samsara or nirvana, is the "excitement" (*rol pa*) or "creativity" (*rtsal*) or "beauty" (*rgyan*) of *bodhicitta* itself.[20] This is not the same as the *Cittamātra* claim that "how things appear is (our) potential for experiencing" (*snang ba sems yin*).

First of all, as we have said, this last statement must be properly understood. In his *Yid bzhin mdzod*, Klong chen pa states:

> One asks whether how things appear is our potential for experience or not, because of such statements (in the sūtras) as, "That which appears is itself an appearance," "O Buddha-sons, the three realms are merely our potential for experience," and "The potential for experience that is stirred up by habituating tendencies gives rise to that which presents itself objectively."[21] One must understand that the statement, "how things appear is experience," which presupposes the distinction between "how things appear" (*snang ba*) and "the thing which is apparent" (*snang yul*), is made because apprehending something as appearing in some way or another is one's own experiencing. The statement, "how things appear is our potential for experiencing," is intended to refute those such as the Śrāvakas and others who, deluded about the objective side of experience, hold it to really exist as they experience it. But mountains, etc., are not thereby shown to be one's own experiencing. One should recognize as experiencing, how something appears when one is caught up in trying to grasp it through thought, such as when one thinks, "Oh, this is a mountain." Therefore, objects that appear, such as mountains,

are not just one's experience, since one finds that their
cause, effect, functioning, origin, and cessation are different
from that of experience. Then, is it as those who hold that
conceptualized objects really exist, claim? The answer is
"no." Those who hold that conceptualized objects really
exist, take the appearing of something as a composite,
material object to be something other than atoms, etc. [i.e.,
mental]. However, we maintain that how things appear is
without root or basis, occasioned by the intoxicant of the
deluding habituating tendencies making themselves felt in
experience. Therefore, we are those who say that there is no
actuality to how things appear. Therefore, the distinction
between how things appear and the thing that appears, is
very important.[22]

This distinction between "how something appears" (*snang
ba*) and the "thing that appears" (*snang yul*) is what may be
called a tacit assumption of Cittamātra thought, which Klong
chen pa is making explicit here. The task which the Yogācāra
philosopher sets for him or herself, as we have said, is to show
that how things appear, how they present themselves, is
nothing but our own experiencing. That is, how things appear
is not produced by an independently existing, objective state
of affairs possessing inherent properties. How things appear
is due to our individual and species-specific karma. The point
of the famous example of the water experienced variously by
the sentient beings of the six realms is that there is no "essence" or "property" that can be attributed to water outside
of the karmically conditioned way of envisioning things that
each of the sentient beings of the six realms have. But Klong
chen pa concludes this passage with a criticism of those who,
while recognizing that our experience of composite, material
objects cannot be accounted for in terms of causes produced
by their "really existing" atomic structure (realism), maintain
that this experience exists as something "nonphysical."

Klong chen pa goes on to explain the understanding of
"how things appear" in the *Sems sde*, in his *Grub mtha'
mdzod* as follows:

The "Mind series" (*Sems sde*) holds that, at bottom, how things appear, in all its variation, is never anything else than the exciting play of the unique fact of awareness, just as there are various appearances, pleasant and unpleasant, on the single surface of a mirror. It holds that, while the way things appear, in all its variation, always presents itself as a specific experience; in fact, it is not anything affirmable, and is not to be divided from the unique fact of awareness. How things appear is then, at bottom, the unique fact of awareness, clear and bright, ever-fresh awareness which owes nothing to extrinsic causes. *The Tantra of the Bright Opening Up of the Total Field Experience (Klong gsal)*[23] states:

"How things appear, in all its variation, is a content of our own experience.
The one awareness, undivided ground, is spoken of as free from drift and dispersion,
As bright clarity, as staying with ever-fresh awareness which owes nothing to extrinsic causes."

Nowadays, ignoramuses say that rDzogs chen claims that how things appear is merely our own experience. This is totally unacceptable, for it leads to the absurd conclusion that experiencing can be divided into parts, colors, and qualities you can get a hold on, since the way things appear seems to be so. Therefore, although how things appear in all its variation, the magic show of what we encounter, in fact, is not real, just like reflections in a mirror, you should know that how things appear to our way of thinking is a property of our habitual tendency to delude ourselves. The unique fact of awareness, the ground of how things appear, is like the surface of a mirror, impartial about what appears in it. You should know that what it comes down to, the flash of knowing which gives awareness its (illumining) quality, is beyond such imaginary boundaries and differences as one/many.[24]

Klong-chen-pa gives a more thorough discussion in his *gNas lugs mdzod*, while explaining the first of the four "commitments" (*dam tshig, samāyā*) or rDzogs chen, "nonexistence" (*med pa*):

Although the way things appear seems something totally independent of experiencing, in the last analysis, it is neither merely our experience nor something other than our experience. As the verse puts it,

> Thus, although all configurations of events/meanings present themselves in experience,
> Since they are neither our experience of them nor something other than it,
> They elude, at any given moment, both speech and thought,
> Like a conjurer's illusion, apparently visible but really nonexistent.
> Therefore, you should know that all configurations of events/meanings that present themselves in experience
> Have not been real from the start,

Since all the configurations of events/meanings that present themselves to us as the five sense objects of visible form, and so forth, as well as the whole outer world and the beings it contains, are present in experience, they are not something apart from the experience. Although they seem to be something other than the experience, since they are actually nonexistent, like a dream or conjurer's illusion, they can't be found as something apart from experience. Also, for this reason, they can't be identified with experience itself, as illustrated by the eight similes of conjurer's illusion, and so forth.[25] Examining the ultimate components, whether individual or composite, of material objects that, although they are nothing at all, are clearly experienced, shows that either way they are just the same in that there is nothing that makes them what they are. Thus, from the specific ways in which the unique fact of awareness presents itself, you can come to know the total field of experience, which opens up continuously but does not split or alter itself.

Well, now, are you saying that everything is merely our experience of it or not? Here I shall make a clear distinction. In general, when I explain that the outer world and the sentient beings it contains, going around in circles (samsara) and going beyond suffering (nirvana), are both what we call being in the state of pure and total presence, this means that they cannot be split off from, nor disrupt, the openness in which the flash of knowing gives awareness its (illumining) quality. That is, we are referring to how they present themselves as the beauty, excitement, or creativity of the flash of awareness, which we can call our experience, in the sense that we refer to the rays of the sun as the sun, or say that there is the sun in a place in a house that receives sunlight.

Fundamentally, there are two faults (to the belief that everything is just our own experience). First, according to reason, there is the absurd conclusion that experience would be present as having parts and color, since what presents itself has parts and color. There would also be the absurd conclusion that since an experience would also be something external and what presents itself also be something internal, everything would become confused. Further, at the time of one's own death, there would be the absurd conclusion that the whole outer world and the beings it contains, would also die, and so forth. Thus, there is the fault according to reason, because the thesis leads to absurd consequences.[26]

Second, there is also the fault of not being in accord with authoritative texts. The *Tantra of the Mirror that is the Primordial Experience of Samantabhadra* (*Kun tu bzang po thugs kyi me long*) states: "Claiming that what presents itself is itself experience, is an obstacle, according to me."[27] The *Tantra of How the Flash of Awareness Presents Itself* (*Rig pa rang shar*) states:

> [Although in reality the potential for experience is without subjective bias, the potential for experience in its relative condition has this subjective bias.] Why does one claim the potential for experience to be relative? Since everything comes about through it, (one speaks of) the potential for experience in its relative condition. Does it also bring about the goal, the state of an Awakened One? [Answer: since everything comes about through it, the state of an Awakened One (also) comes about through it.] . . .
> [Since there is no duality in the ground of being, how can one claim there is duality? We shall answer this question as follows: in the ground of being where there are neither Awakened Ones nor sentient beings, there is neither two-ness nor three-ness. Through the

creativity of its exciting energy, Awakened Ones and sentient beings come about. Now (in this case) one can believe that the ground of being is dual. Therefore, one speaks of the existence of duality. Since there is no good or bad in the ground of being, there is no change.] Therefore, it is logical that sentient beings cannot become Awakened Ones.

For example, although one cleans black charcoal, it won't become white; in the same way, although deluded sentient beings practice meditation, they won't become Awakened Ones.[28]

The *Tantra that Sums Up the Real Meaning (Nges don 'dus pa'i rgyud)* states:

Stupid people, who do not see the real meaning, say that what presents itself is one's own experience. This is like taking brass as gold.

Here nowadays, some people proud of their knowledge of rDzogs chen and some followers of the ordinary, *sūtra* approach to the teachings, claim that what presents itself is one's own experience. Without making (necessary) distinctions they speak erroneously. "Experience," and "being in a state of pure and total presence" are not the same. "Experience" is the accidental impurity that is the eight modes of awareness belonging to the three life-worlds, together with their specific functions.[29] The "state of pure and total presence" is the flash of knowing that gives awareness its quality, ever-fresh awareness that owes nothing to extrinsic causes, the total field of all going around in circles (samsara) and going beyond suffering (nirvana), without characteristics by which to define it, or substance. Here, in this teaching, since the outer world and the living beings it contains present themselves as the creativity and excitement of the state of pure and total presence, the "state of pure and total presence" is simply a name for the cause of freedom using the word for the result.[30] Through knowing that that which comes forth as samsara and nirvana is the creativity of the flash of knowing that gives awareness its quality, you can understand that the flash of knowing itself is the unceasing basis of that which presents itself, although it is itself neither samsara nor nirvana.

You should know that how things present themselves as an obvious object without, however, being concrete, is in fact pure and ever-fresh, has no cause, is lucent and transparent, and is neither within nor outside of experience. Since the energies we are calling "excitement" and "creativity" just are (with no cause or aim), then ultimate freedom is as spontaneous as shedding a dream when one awakens. That which liberates itself drops away its apparent substance and characteristics, without moving away from where it belongs and has always been. It has always been with that flash of knowing that gives awareness its quality, which is itself continuing communication with the total field of events and meanings.

Nowadays, there is no one except myself who makes this distinction; there are only those who claim that what presents itself is an experience and those who claim it is something apart from the experience. In this case, even our own school (the rNying ma pa) has not understood, since they assert that the presence of the energies of creativity and excitement that enhance the flash of knowing, are at bottom the same. In this regard, you should know that "creativity" is the capacity of the flash of knowing that gives awareness its quality, to come forth as samsara and nirvana, just as one ray of sunlight makes the lotus open and the water-lily close. "Excitement" is the play of the flash of knowing as it shimmers, like the play of sun or lamplight. "Beauty" means that when visibility presents itself, it enhances the flash of knowing which arises on its own, just as the sky is enriched by a rainbow or made splendid by the sun, moon, and stars. These energies are spoken of in the *Tantra of the Bright Opening Up of the Field of Experience*, which speaks of:

. . . creativity without interruption,
and,
  I teach that the very being of (the energy called) 'excitement' is linked up with uninterrupted non-duality,
and,
  Therefore, it is said, enhanced by beauty.

We are finished with this overlong discussion.[31]

Finally, in his *Chos dbyings mdzod*, Klong chen pa also discusses the problem of *Sems sde* and *Sems tsam* directly:

Those who are not graced by high learning and speak of the "method of spontaneity,"[32] claim that the way things appear in their objective variety is the state of pure and total presence, which is one's own mind. But here (in the *Sems sde*), the teaching that (the variety of how things appear) is actually one in the expanse of the state of pure and total presence, is very different, abysmally so. These stupid people take the state of pure and total presence to be their own (ordinary) experiencing, but here we hold that (our ordinary experiencing) presents itself through the creativity of the ongoing state of pure and total presence that has been apprehended as a "subject." The way things appear has always been a radiance not existing internally nor externally apart from being a mere play of the creativity (of pure and total presence). It is not found as something mental or other than mental, but is held to be merely how things present themselves interdependently when secondary conditions are present. . . .

Your claim that explains everything as mental is not the same as that of the *Sems sde*. The *Sems sde* speaks in terms of everything arising from the state of pure and total presence and appearing playfully from the creativity of that (state). Using an analysis into three categories—"state of pure and total presence," "excitement," and "creativity"— all configurations of events and meanings can be situated. The "state of pure and total presence" is like the sky, since it encompasses everything, without itself being anything in particular. "Creativity" is like the surface of a polished mirror, always responsive to whatever presents itself. "Excitement," as in the eight examples of illusion, refers to the variations of that which presents itself. Since these three, moreover, in their aspect of being an open dimension, are not found as anything, they are nondual. But in their aspect of how they appear, they appear as the triad of the state of pure and total presence, excitement, and creativity, conventionally speaking. They have actually always been nondual, while appearing one from the other, as the flash of knowing, sleep, and dream (appear one from the other).[33] These are, in fact, beyond the labels of one and many, while in view of how they appear, they are explained conventionally as three.

According to a conventional analysis, that is, according

to how they appear, we cannot, in fact, accept the state of pure and total presence and its excitement as one. Therefore, we can make the distinction between how things appear and that which appears in view of these energies of excitement. Thus we can understand the eight similes of the apparitional, reflectionlike quality, etc., of how things appear while not existing as anything internal or external. Because of this understanding, although one postulates a subject and its qualities, etc., one should thoroughly comprehend them as primordially nonexistent yet clearly apparent, this being the claim of this rDzogs chen system.[34] Understanding this explanation one has entered into the specific superiority (of rDzogs chen) over other philosophical systems, since there exist many analyses of samsara and nirvana, etc., which are distinctive, subtle, and comprehensive. Nowadays, only our own system has this excellent explanation.[35]

A key image here is that of the mirror. The Yogācāra analysis, one might say, is at the level of the reflections (*sems*), which are all relative and interdependent. "Experiencing" means that one finds oneself in the relative, within the limits of time and action, in which one can be said to be "creating" one's actions through the three "gates" of body, speech, and mind, as traditionally analyzed in all Buddhist schools. But *bodhicitta*, or *sems nyid*, "primordial experiencing," is like the surface of the mirror. The reflections are not the mirror surface, but neither can the reflections be separated from the reflecting capacity of the mirror surface. They are its *rol pa*, its fascinating manifestations, although the mirror surface does not act to create the reflections.

Now, if we follow out the logic of this example, then from the very beginning there is nothing to accept or reject, purify or transform, since the mirror is not in the least bit tainted, changed, or conditioned by any reflection in it. Hence one speaks of "total completeness" (*rDzogs chen*). In the Bodhisattva path of the Mahāyāna, for example, such a state is regarded as belonging to the goal, i.e., "Buddhahood," while the basis or starting point is established and the path traversed by means of acceptance and rejection, i.e., accepting those aspects of experience that are conducive to liberation and rejecting those experienced as noncónducive.

Does rDzogs chen hold that there is literally nothing to do, that the goal is literally present in the individual? How is the understanding of the inherent purity (*ka dag*) of the mirror surface actually implemented? It is at this point that we must turn to the meditation instructions given by Mañjuśrīmitra that accompany the *Byang chub sems bsgom pa*. Here, it is of crucial importance to understand the method specific to rDzogs chen, "self-liberation," "intrinsic freedom" (*rang grol*).[36] It is through this method that there is, rightly understood, "nothing to do."

III

Meditation
The Oral Instructions of Mañjuśrīmitra

IN THE *Vairocana 'rGyud 'bum* there is a text on the practice of meditation based on the *Byang chub sems bsgom pa*, entitled *Byang chub sems bsgom pa'i bsam gtan rna mar rgyud (kyi man ngag)*, "the oral instruction that is a tantra on the practice of cultivating the state of pure and total presence," attributed to Mañjuśrīmitra. We here translate it to round out the picture that our text provides of the *Sems sde* tradition.[1]

As regards meditation in rDzogs chen, the crucial question one has to ask is: how does one actually *practice* nonaction? Is this not a contradiction in terms? Now, we know that using the (activity of the) mind to go beyond the mind is a traditional theme in Buddhism. "Not-doing" is a fundamental concept of Taoism resonant with Chinese Ch'an (Zen) Buddhism: the Sage "acts without acting." But how is this made a reality? Or, to put it another way, in terms of the two major misunderstandings of nonaction: how is it to be prevented from degenerating into either remaining passive and indifferent (in fact, avoiding activity), on the one hand; or into doing whatever comes to mind under the guise of a doctrine of spontaneity (which does not, in fact, deal with the basic problem of one's deep-seated conditions, all one's habits and passions), on the other? Nonaction is basically the discovery of *freedom* as something inseparable from our *being*; it cannot be created. In this respect, freedom is not the opposite of determinism but of compulsion, of *having* to act.[2] Both of the above mentioned extremes remain tied to a concept: one holds to the idea of being calm, of being in a state of meditation; while the other holds to the idea of being free from all limitations by waging war against one's limits.

First of all, it should be understood that nonaction has two aspects, as discussed in our text: as "meditation" (*sgom pa, bhavanā*) and as "behavior" (*spyod pa, cārya*), these two being based on the first of this traditional triad—*lta ba, drsti,* "philosophical outlook," "self-observation." That is, based on the outlook or point of view of a teaching, a practice of meditation can be set up, and this will also lead to a certain way of acting in the world. Here a spontaneous, unpremeditated way of acting, in which one does not have to avoid any situation as negative, for example, is only possible having had some experience of "nondoing" as meditation. This meditation is a profound grasp of the "natural condition" of the mind, usually termed *rig pa*. Only in this natural condition can there be "nondoing." Now, in additioin to "nonaction," *natural* is another much abused term which seems to have lost any real meaning. But here "natural" is re-endowed with meaning because it is based on a precise experience. We can point to this experience by words such as "inalienable" and "uncontrived." "Natural" refers to the "ultimate content" (*chos nyid, dharmatā*) of what we call our "mind." In this condition, or rather noncondition, there is nothing to correct or adjust, accept or reject; there is no meditation to enter into or come out of. Thus one can speak of "self-liberation" (*rang grol*) in rDzogs chen: as said before, nothing need be done to experience freedom. "Freedom" means that there is no possibility for positive or negative thoughts or actions to condition the individual (that is, set up the habituating tendencies discussed in the previous section), who "rests in" his/her own inalienable "nature."

In this *man ngag*, or oral instruction, as in all the *Sems sde* teachings, much emphasis is laid on finding a state of "relaxation" in which one is not disturbed by whatever thoughts may arise, or in which there is an actual absence of thoughts. This is technically termed *gnas pa'i rnal 'byor*, the first of the four "yogas" (*rnal 'byor*) which characterize the *Sems sde* teaching,[3] and is very similar to the well-known practice of *zhi gnas*, *śamatha*, "state of calm."

In sutric Buddhism, however, *zhi gnas* is generally regarded as a kind of prerequisite for entering into the practice of *lhag mthong*, *vipaśyanā*, "insight," which is itself regarded as a kind of analytical meditation, like shining a searchlight on objects, one by one, in a dark room.[4] But rDzogs chen is not a "gradual," but a "direct" path, i.e., the fundamental conception is not one of a graded series of steps towards the goal, although the "four yogas" of *Sems sde* are presented in a quasi-gradual manner, so that the *Sems sde* seems like a gradual path in relation to the other two series of rDzogs chen teachings, the *klong sde* and the *man ngag sde*.[5] In this case, *zhi gnas* means to enter, if one has the capacity, not merely a state of calm that makes possible further, more refined, mental "work," but the primordial state of relaxation spoken of earlier, the "resting in" (*gnas pa*) one's inalienable nature. As the *man ngag* states:

"Relaxation" (*lhug pa*) means, in this regard, that one doesn't necessarily sit cross-legged, etc.; that there is neither distraction nor stupefaction of the senses; and that in whatever situation one is in (there is) the intrinsic clarity of the state of pure and total presence, without entering into an attitude of correcting the condition of the body and the senses.[6]

This practice is stabilized by doing one's "sessions of meditation" (*thun*) in an unforced manner, by unfolding one's relaxation, as it were, through giving oneself space to relax. Hence the length of a session is never fixed, and emphasis is placed on self-regulation. If one's sessions are forced, one suffocates oneself, and thus can never find an uncontrived state.

Another important topic in this oral instruction on meditation is what is termed *nyams*, or the experiential signs of the development of practice. These signs arise as the process of relaxation takes place. Relaxation has not been possible before because the individual has constantly charged himself up, so that the three levels of his existence—body, speech and mind[7]—have become extremely sensitive and reactive to one another. The signs are usually grouped according to the three types of experiences much utilized in Tantrism: that of pleasurable sensation (*bde ba*), clarity (*gsal ba*), and absence of disturbing thoughts (*mi rtog pa*).[8] In rDzogs chen it is fundamental to recognize the difference between the *nyams* and *rig pa*, which is the state of pure and total presence in which these various experiences are reflected, as in a mirror. As the text states:

> A manifestation of clarity should not be taken to be the ultimate content of what is. Therefore, one relaxes without attachment to the ultimate content of what is, or to delight in the experiences of absence of body, speech, and mind.[9]

The state of calm is itself a *nyams*, an experience characterized by the absence of disturbing thoughts (*mi rtog pa*), and is thus only a means to enter *rig pa*, our primordial, inalienable, natural state (which is both "being" and "knowing" inseparably united). Then, in this state one can understand how it is possible to behave in such a manner as to act without acting, where one does not *have to* avoid anything nor *have to* dwell on anything. Otherwise, as mentioned above, if one imagines one is being spontaneous by following whatever comes into one's head, one is just *trying* to be free. The essential point is total relaxation in which there is no compulsion to accept (give in to) or reject one's deep-seated conditioning. Thus one finds the ongoing reality of "self-liberation," the natural state.

ORAL INSTRUCTIONS ON CONTEMPLATION
ACCORDING TO
Cultivating the State of Pure and Total Presence

Having completed the preliminaries to be realized, the superior individual, one who transfers all sentient beings into the state of liberation, so commits himself, with the intention of great compassion, to transfer all sentient beings to full liberation. Then, by bringing together the necessary conditions, the individual who knows what places of true solitude and places of distraction (such as cities, places of entertainment, marketplaces, etc.,) are, firmly decides (the direction of his or her existence) by satisfying the teacher according to this text, *Cultivating the State of Pure and Total Presence.*

Regarding the meaning of practice, there are two aspects to (the practice of) leaving the mind in each moment in a pure state, even if there is no mental activity: erroneous (practice) and correct (practice). Erroneous practice is spoken of in these lines:

> Having eliminated holding on to form, identifiable characteristics, and wishfulness, while cultivating the three "gateways to freedom,"[10]
> Is the activity of the Lord of limitations. Form itself is open-dimensional.
> Eliminating the three paths of samsara while cultivating nirvana is also the activity of the Lord of limitations.
>
> [104–6]

A practitioner who is bound by the subject-object dichotomy cultivates openness through having abandoned form, cultivates the absence of identifiable characteristics through abandoning characteristics, and cultivates the absence of desire by abandoning desire. This is the activity of the Lord of limitations, which does not allow one to see the true meaning (of practice), since one falls into the extremes of acceptance and rejection. Moreover, the superior individual does not cultivate nonattachment, kindness, and the clarity of ever-

fresh awareness through abandoning attachment, aversion, and dullness. That, too, would be the activity of the Lord of limitations.
Well, then, how should one practice? The body should first be taken care of. Then when the time for practice arrives, one's bodily condition will not be disturbed. The superior individual knows the conditions necessary for contemplation. It is said in the basic text,

> Grasping experience through thought, which is the sphere of operation of our "mind," is itself the ultimate content of what is.
> Since one is free from (seizing on) perceptible qualities, there does not exist anything that is better or worse. This supreme path is to be cultivated.   [112–113]

Therefore one does not engage in affirmation or negation, knowing that there is nothing to accept or reject.
Moreover, according to the meaning of the lines,

> One does not remain even in the states of the absence of movement of thought or of nonmovement.   [102]
> One should not remain in a state wherein there is no doubt, nor eliminate a state of doubt.   [90]

One knows that there should be no preoccupation with body, speech, and mind, although the body is seated in the seven-point (Vairocana posture) on a comfortable seat, talking is stopped, and the mind is held calm. That is, body, speech, and mind are left relaxed and nothing is corrected. "Relaxation" means, in this regard, that one doesn't necessarily sit cross-legged, etc.; that there is neither distraction nor stupefication of the senses; and that whatever situation one is in, the intrinsic clarity of pure and total presence (is present) without entering into an attitude of correcting the condition of the body and the senses. There is also no meditative attention to thought or nonthought; even the state of absence of objects is not objectified; and the state of not dwelling on anything is not itself dwelled upon. One doesn't get involved with even the slightest notion of accepting this or rejecting that. One does not cultivate the path to nirvana while rejecting the path of samsara, with its concepts, faults, states of calm, and objects of meditation. Through becoming aware of the absence of any thought whatsoever, one naturally settles into a state of not dwelling on any notion, even that of not thinking, nor does one slip under the power of drowsiness or lack of presence, nor does one become agitated. Therefore, freedom from all notions is the direct reflexive knowledge that is the flash of knowing that gives awareness its (illumining) quality.[11] This reflexive flash of knowing presents itself nonconceptually without rejecting (anything).

Further, the *Tantra on Cultivating the State of Pure and Total Presence*[12] states, speaking about the position (of the body and senses):

> Without separating object and sense, relax their spheres of operation.
> The Awakened Ones arises from this relaxation of the senses in which (no thoughts) remain hidden (from awareness).

Also, regarding how one leaves the mind be, it says:

> One doesn't dwell even in the "middle," there being no middle since there are no extremes. Without dwelling on anything whatsoever, in such a way should one cultivate a state of calm. Since the total field of events and meanings is without center or periphery, there is no way to indicate it by name. As-it-is-ness, which is the real sense of this absence of indication, is to be attended to without conception of self or other. If something objectifiable exists, the Awakened One does not seek it. The meaning of "not seeking" is that (such an object) is just one's own mind, and in such a way should one cultivate a state of calm.

A manifestation of clarity should not be taken to be the ultimate content of what is. Therefore, one relaxes without attachment to the ultimate content of what is, or to delight in the experiences of absence of body, speech, and mind. Further, since one is beyond the objects of thought, there is no seeking or making an object out of the ultimate content of what is, where there is no (deceptive) appearance. Thus one practices a state of calm.

Arriving in fact at one's natural condition is spoken of in the three lines:

> Since neither do conditioned events arise (on their own)
> nor do all configurations of events and meanings come
> about (dependently), all these are taken beyond the realm
> of frustration and suffering.
> When (one has thoroughly grasped) that there are no "en-
> tities," everything then (arises) as the total field of events
> and meanings—understanding this is the supreme state
> of those who have overcome emotional conflicts.
> Space is unobjectifiable and is a mere name. That which is
> positive (for an individual) and that which is negative,
> being indivisible, do not arise.   [114–116]

Regarding the knowledge of arriving, in fact, at the natural condition of the mind in practice, and of how the experiential signs of practice develop, (the first) is that there is not even the notion of thought or no thought, since there is, in fact, neither an origination nor cessation of thought. In (this state where) one is not distracted and does not objectify (one's experience), one does not slip under the power of agitation or sleepiness. There is no experiencing (mind) that can be pointed out. Since not experiencing any signs of successful practice is real experience, the tantra says:

> If one is attached to the clarity of one's mental condition,
> When, in a certain moment, there is a profound (experi-
> ence) of the absence of thought,
> That is not thorough comprehension, since a profound ex-
> perience
> In which there is no thought, is still an experience.

The stages of development (of the experiential signs of successful practice) are: the experiential sign of "movement" is both the wandering and diffusion of mind, which give rise to agitation and lack of mental presence; the experiential sign of "accustoming (oneself to the practice)" is that, while coarse thoughts do not arise, there are subtle ones that are liberated (merely) by experiencing them, in that they do not have the power to impede (practice); the experiential sign that practice is "stabilized" is that one's awareness is not conditioned by objects. (Here) the flashing forth of the knowledge that gives awareness its quality, which does not enter within any objective condition, flows like a river, and there is no opportunity to grasp at experience through thoughts.

Making corrections when one recognizes defects in the practice is indicated by the line:

> As long as there is the agitated movement of the mind,
> there is the realm of the Lord of limitations.　　　　[101]

Because of this one should recognize the following: the six distractions; the five impediments; the arising of the five poisons; the eighteen obstacles; the seven defects; the ten impediments; the defect of accepting or rejecting what one feels obligated to do through body, speech, or mind; the eighteen spheres of operation of the Lord of limitations, etc; as well as impediments due to concrete objects or to thoughts of past, present, or future at the time of practice.[13] Although there is nothing about these to reject, provisionally, what is called "correcting the mind" refers to the nonarising of thoughts (of acceptance and rejection), since one does not engage in accepting or rejecting.

There is, moreover, the correcting of the body and vocal energy, as well as the mind. These can be done erroneously or correctly. Error refers to correcting because of a subtle attachment to the three gates. The tantra states:

> There is nothing to be affirmed and nothing to dwell on;
> Since there is no conditioned activity, (knowing it) is like knowing space;
> Therefore, everything arising from conditioned activity is a defect of contemplation.

And further,

> Experiencing itself cannot be objectified or dwelled upon.
> Removing this defect of objectifying and dwelling on ex-
>   perience
> Is a subtle form of mental fixation.

And further,

> In the same way, sitting cross-legged with back straight
> And fixing one's mind on reality,
> Correcting one's bodily position as one wishes—
> These come from attachment to the body.

Eliminating unconducive elements (to practice) and affirming pleasing ones is like being tied to a post, as it is said,

> Correcting body and mind according to what pleases one
> Is the peg by which thoughts are held.

Correct [practice] is indicated by the line

> When [a thought] arises one does not eliminate it, nor does
>   one construct a support for the mind when no (thought)
>   arises.   [109]

One does not necessarily reject thoughts that arise nor con-struct a support for the mind when thoughts don't arise. The ultimate content of what is does not manifest as any experi-ence of clarity. Therefore, it is said,

> [Even if] there stirs the slightest (thought) that is not (the
>   dimension of knowledge called) Mañjuśrī, this itself is
>   still that (dimension). But one does not try to remain in
>   that.   [110]

Since even the subtlest thought that may arise is the "ultimate content of what is" presenting itself, there is nothing to cor-rect. Thus, someone who knows this, knows that thought is the exciting play (of the primordial state of pure and total presence) that gives rise to ever-fresh awareness, and thus has no obstacles. Therefore, there is neither a meditator nor something to be meditated upon; the understanding of their indivisible unity is the supreme (practice) because (thoughts of correcting) do not arise in that there is nothing whatsoever to correct. Also, it is said,

> If an experience, just like the object that is its "cause," does not exist concretely,
> Then nothing can be objectified or dwelt upon. What activity can there be?
> Just as the sky has nothing about it to be corrected, so also for the body.
> If you know that your body is like an apparition
> There is also no sitting cross-legged, with back straight, to be done.
> Whatever is taken as an object of the three spheres of activity
> One does not have to act upon—from the beginning there is nothing to be done.

And,

> Since you know the nature of what presents itself in experience as its objective cause,
> There is nothing to correct there.

Naturally arising self-liberation is also of two kinds.[14] The first, naturally arising self-liberation involving a mental commitment, is that, as soon as one experiences a defect in one's practice, without blocking it one then relaxes. Since the defect then does not arise later, one speaks of its self-liberation. Then, naturally arising self-liberation not involving a mental commitment is that, as soon as a thought arises, without blocking or acting on it, through a previously existing profound understanding, that thought itself becomes the "ultimate content of what is" presenting itself, and is thus self-liberated. For example, like a thief who flees upon discovery, or like adding wood to a fire, as soon as the thought is experienced it presents itself as ever-fresh awareness. So, although there is nothing to meditate on, one speaks of meditation that is naturally nondistracted. Judgments of truth and untruth do not arise; seeing anything as a fault or positive quality ceases; and one does not fall away from what is really so: this is the supreme intent. Also, the following verse explains the meaning of the word (*contemplation*):

> The reflexive flash of knowing that gives awareness its
>   quality eludes speech and thought,
> And is indivisible from the unthinkable total field of experience.
> To settle thus in this unthinkable flashing of knowing that
>   gives awareness its quality
> Is called the "contemplation that enters that which is, as it
>   is."

Therefore, there is no regret, aversion, or envy regarding thoughts that arise, nor is there attachment to the ultimate content of what is.

Gauging the duration of a session of practice is as follows: people of superior constitution and intelligence, from the time they begin practice until it is stabilized, can sleep contentedly at night, and then, when waking should practice their sessions of meditation during the day without staying in one place. Then, when this (practice) has been stabilized, they should practice at dawn, dusk, and in the evening. During the day one can do four sessions of practice, three in the morning and one in the afternoon. At dusk, when the energy is right, one should practice. Then, after, one can lengthen the sessions, and one will be able to stay in a state of calm for half a day, and then half a month or a month. In general, when one sees that there are no interruptions in the sessions, during a twenty-four-hour period, one can do eight short sessions of practice during the daytime and rest calmly at night. When one experiences disturbances of one's condition, reduce the length of the session and fortify oneself with some food. Then, if the disturbance increases, leave off practicing and cure it.

The length of a session should be about twenty minutes, or it can be the time it takes to do twenty inhalation-exhalations. Then, if one is free from drowsiness or nervousness, one can double the length of the session, or according to how one feels one can increase it by half or a third gradually, learning not to suffocate oneself. Then, through accustoming oneself (to the practice), the duration of a session can last 10,000 inhalation-exhalations. About forty to fifty minutes can be the length of a session. When one is able, during the daytime one can do three sessions, and also practice in the early morning and evening. In short, one should regulate the length of a session according to one's condition, and practice in short sessions respecting one's condition. Having stabilized the practice, one can add half the amount of time (to a session) without suffocating oneself. A session that is not disturbed by defects of practice gives rise to the (experiential sign of) "stability," clarity, and longer sessions. One should practice gauging the just measure that gives rise to these, just as the waning moon begins to wax, and one day follows another. With sessions of mixed length one can slowly stabilize one's experience. At the beginning one should learn from experienced people. Thus, although it seems that one is making efforts, if one understands that there is no effort involved, one won't notice any effort.

The means by which behavior is skillfully conducted is indicated by,

> Just as the "Lotus-like Lord" of everything worldly does not reject anything, [all things] are seen as alike and present in utter sameness, [95]

and by the following three lines,

> If anything positive for the individual, whatever it may be, has not been taken up by the way of acting [symbolized by] Samantabhadri,
>
> Then the way of acting (symbolized by) Samantabhadra becomes the activity of the Lord of limitations—in which case it will reach its limit and be exhausted.[15]
>
> On the path that possesses this (primordial state of pure and total presence), even the activity of the Lord of limitations is said to be the activity of this pure and total presence. [129-131]

Being in a state of Atiyoga contemplation, one acts and trains oneself in "Samantabhadri activity," which is the appreciative discernment that does not turn anything into an object. When one is engaged in the four activities of sleeping, standing, walking, and lying down, one allows for all actions; while during a session of genuine contemplation, one leaves in a state of equanimity all movements of thought that distract and dull concentration, there being no basis for rejecting them. Since a mind that does not objectify anything does not conceive any specific intention, one acts naturally without premeditation. The tantra says:

> From the river of nonaction no experiential signs of practice arise.

And,

> It is necessary to really practice so that everything is spontaneously whole, complete.
> Therefore, one can enjoy sitting, walking, standing, and lying down without premeditation.

A person of superior capacity from the start can do all these together without any premeditation. All those of middling and low capacity, having stabilized their experience a bit, just remain with the thought of having no premeditation whatsoever. Thus, whatever one does, there is no premeditation whatsoever. Practice that is mixed with thought is not at all obscured by thinking. While one is learning, outside of the sessions do not think that what happens is apart from meditation.

A practitioner who acts thusly, even when he/she experiences suffering, does not think: "Oh, poor me, how I suffer! What can I do! I am powerless, without help. I suffer terrible misery while others are happy. Now I am suffering!" Although one experiences suffering, one should think: "Ordinary people, without real understanding, dislike suffering and like happiness. But by accepting happiness and rejecting unhappiness, they have wandered until now (in samsara). I do not reject unhappiness and desire happiness, since both are without any actuality. Since the self does not exist, suffering is also a wave of the ultimate content of what is." Thinking of suffering as the ultimate content of what is (which is nothing at all), the person who does not think (of it) as suffering takes hold of the intention of Samantabhadra. Since hell is understood to be the state of an Awakened One and the narrow passage of samsara is seen to be a pleasant place, don't think about momentary worldly suffering but think in the long term. Therefore, whatever pleasure or pain arises while engaging in walking, standing, sleeping, and lying down, one acts without acting, without premeditating anything. The tantra says:

> Do not think that not thinking about anything is also "that which is, as it is."
> Do not cultivate the state of an Awakened One; abandon deities; abandon all spheres of operation of the mind.
> Do not use a *vajra* or any mantra or ritual material.
> Do not stay in an isolated place.
> Do not make any offerings of *gtor ma* and gifts, nor dedicate (any merit). For who is there to dedicate it to?
> Do not engage in any disturbing practices such as rituals.
> That is total completeness, the core of how everything actually is. But in this there is nothing whatsoever.

Here, since everything is complete in the flash of knowing that rests in total equanimity, there is no need to do things one by one. Therefore, until you have attained a contemplation that is able to enter into all activities, you should reject all "doing." Whatever you do, do not go outside of what is intended (by this). Having obtained the ability (to bring contemplation into action), then, without cutting off activity, there is no activity.

How the indications of being in a state of contemplation for a long time, which are the experiences of "warmth,"[16] will manifest is uncertain. Internal indications of "warmth" are: the breath is easy and even so subtle as not to be felt; or during the session the movement of the mind is stopped; or the movement of the mind is stopped for a long time. External indications are: although one remains for a long time in a fixed position, illness, odors, and vermin are not present, and one's condition is that of pleasure. Internally, when one remains in a state of equanimity, one will have a vision of the atoms (of the body), etc. The "secret" indication is that the mind is happy, there is no effort, and the mind arrives at its natural condition, in which all existence appears as it is but one cannot describe this experience.

The indications are indicated by the verse:

> One's mind is not engaged in seeking anything. One is not disturbed by anything, knowing the fundamental alikeness [of everything].   [120]

How do the indications arise with practice? Although one sees a celestial damsel or the form of a Victorious One, one is not attached; although one sees the Lord of limitations or a demoness, fear and aversion do not arise; one does not experience these with any sense of concreteness; although there are obstructing conditions one is not separated from contemplation, nor does one construct a support for the mind; and when the mind is in a state of contemplation it is not conditioned by any external object whatsoever. Further, the tantra states:

> Although one sees the embodied form of an Awakened One or is among the Noble Ones, one is not attached.
> Although one sees demons and demonesses, etc., and the Hell of Wind, aversion does not arise.
> Contemplation comes about from fully grasping and understanding the nature of such (experiences),
> And the absence of attachment to the experience of contemplation comes about from the absence of acceptance and rejection, in which there is no grasping after experience through thought whatsoever.

In short, one is not attached to even transworldly pleasure; one does not fear even the abyss of hell; one is not disgusted even by the activity of the Lord of limitations; one is not averse to negative conditions; one is not proud of the presence of positive qualities. Since there is no self and other, jealousy does not arise. Although one is in accord with everyone, one is not attached. Whatever suffering arises, the mind is not conditioned by it. Such a person is called a "Buddhason." One speaks of "accumulation (of merit and knowledge)," having purified one's obstacles and extended the experiential sign of "stability" that acts as a "cause," as follows:

> The mind is not engaged in seeking nor is it directed towards anything. One is free from knowing and not knowing.
> There is neither picking out nor attending to (aids to meditation).[17] Delight in acceptance and rejection are alike in not existing. Not objectifying (anything) and
> Remaining with the (understanding of) this alikeness, there is no creation of duality; one is beyond the realm of speech; there is neither activity nor inactivity; there is no accumulation (of merit) or diminution (of faults), etc.   [117–19]

No effort; no intention; no directing the mind towards an object; freedom from thoughts about particular objects of knowledge; freedom from the dullness of ignorance; no attentiveness, since the ultimate content of what is, like the sky, cannot be objectified; no divisiveness; no relishing any object; no comparison with anything; no dwelling on anything, as well as no dwelling even on nondwelling; no objectification even of nonobjectification; abiding in utter sameness; no imagination of duality; freedom from speech and thought; no action or nonaction while performing actions; no desire to diminish faults or increase the accumulation of merit; no going beyond the natural condition of body, speech, and mind: the signs of stability in unerring, effortless meditation are sixteen.

Impediments having purified themselves through this, the accumulation of merit completes itself effortlessly. Further, experiences of openness, clarity, and pleasure all together, as well as the nonengagement of the mind in conceptualizing objects, indicate the nonwavering state that is the final experiential sign of practice. One can prolong these even for a half-day. When one is able to remain thus as long as possible, one will see concretely the eighteen objects of the Lord of limitations. Since these are manifestations of one's own mind and there is no attachment, one knows that they are the magical play of the ultimate content of what is.

As to impediments:[18] although, as above, there is nothing to purify, if we make a bit of an explanation to please the practitioner, we can say that the emotional impediment is the taking of one's personality as an enduring entity, which is the concept of a "subject." The cognitive impediment is the taking of configurations of events and meanings as enduring entities, which is the concept of an "object." Briefly, the impediment of knowledge is known as "ignorance of the flash of knowing in which (however) the pervasive conflicting emotions are not present." That is, the conflicting emotions are nonexistent, but there is a subtle objectification of the ultimate content of what is itself. In this advanced yoga, since all configurations of events and meanings are from the very beginning the way in which the flash of knowing that gives awareness its quality presents itself as a spontaneous ever-fresh awareness, configurations of events and meanings, taken as entities, cannot be proven as an object apart (from the flash of knowing). Since the mind itself also, in fact, cannot be made into an object, then, when the person as an entity cannot be proven, how can the impediment of the conflicting emotions exist? In that the five conflicting emotions are themselves, in fact, the five forms of ever-fresh awareness,[19] there is nothing to be purified. The ultimate content of what is is not an object of experience, and even this very nonobjectification cannot be made into an object of the intellect, so there is no impediment of knowledge to be purified. Only this is the great direct, reflexive knowledge that is the flash of knowing that gives awareness its quality. Therefore, the tantra also says:

In this there is no impediment to remove; one behaves the same way towards everything.

The positive qualities of having practiced are as follows. Since one has fully understood the nonduality of self and other, knowledge of other minds arises.[20] Since one has fully understood the fundamental alikeness of the three times, there appears the heightened awareness that remembers what happened in previous lives and the heightened awareness that knows the birth and death of beings. Since forms and sounds are thoroughly understood to be the all-inclusive state of the individual, the heightened awareness of godlike sight and hearing arises. Further, the manifestation of miracles[21] comes about from the power of the full grasp that there is nothing that makes things what they are. The manifestation of visions arises from the thorough understanding that whatever presents itself is unobstructed. Miraculous abilities of prophecy arise from obtaining a heightened awareness of sound and from the knowledge of other minds. Miraculous abilities associated with speech arise from understanding all sounds as the way in which the flash of knowing that gives awareness its quality communicates itself. But going beyond the commonly understood sense of these (we can say): through the power of this meditation in which all inner and outer configurations of events and meanings are spontaneously present, one's impediments clarify themselves without having to act on them, and these positive qualities manifest themselves like a reflection in clear water. In one who possesses such a profound reality, there will also be relics and various manifestations after death. The tantra says:

> In the depths of the mind of (s)he who possesses this reality
> there will be equality with all the Awakened Ones.
> As to the body, relics will appear.

Although there is no obtaining a fruit of meditation, one who purifies the impediments to his/her own intrinsic state of awakeness merely makes fully present his own state. In this

there is no attainment through outer activities. Further, since
the tantra says,

> Having completely liberated the three realms and purified
>   the six forms of sentient beings, there is the intrinsic state
>   of awakeness.
> The Victorious Awakened Ones do not exist apart from
>   this. This is the truth.

There is nothing to be obtained. Ever-fresh awareness is the
culmination of the power of contemplation, and the outcome
of long meditation on the primordial state of pure and total
presence, which is the ultimate content of what is and Mañjuśrī. We may also refer to it as "primordial contact with the
total field of events and meanings" and the "eye of discernment." Speaking of the attainment of these, the specific positive qualities connected with cultivating the ongoing primordial state of pure and total presence are given in verses such
as:

> When a perceptive person has made this noble, pure and
>   total presence real,
> It is then what the Victorious Ones have spoken of as
>   "primordial contact with the total field of events and
>   meanings," most excellent of the three forms of pri-
>   mordial contact with reality.
> It is also called the "eye of discernment" because of the
>   excellence of its knowing capacity.
> Nonconceptual, ever-fresh awareness, supreme and indes-
>   tructible, is, moreover, also this very (state of pure and
>   total presence),   [10–13]

as well as,

> Since all that can be said to be an aspect of the state of
>   freedom of any of the Noble Ones
> Comes about through the state of pure and total presence
>   reaching its fullness, these capacities arise from that.
> Also, all of those heroically committed to the primordial
>   state of pure and total presence, belonging to the death-
>   less, great, noble lineage,

Could not come into being if this (pure and total presence)
did not exist. Therefore, it is the very path of supreme
freedom.   [14–17]

Thus, practitioners who at present possess fortunate circumstances and an opportunity (to follow this path), by really
remaining in contemplation without doubts, thus abandon all
actions. If one so remains, all that one desires will be inciden-
tally realized and one will continue in the supreme contemplation through obtaining, right now, without acquiring anything, the absolutely complete state of awakeness.

> Yamāntaka[22] is the self-originating deity, lord of all.
> Mañjuśrī, the ultimate content of what is, is nothing other
>   than one's own capacity to experience.

The lordly Mañjuśrīmitra has brought forth such a realization out of the continuum of primordial experience, and set it
down as a treasure for the fortunate ones.

*The Instruction That Is the Spoken Tantra
on Cultivating the Primordial State
of Pure and Total Presence*
IS HEREBY COMPLETED.

THE TEXT

The Verses

CULTIVATING THE PRIMORDIAL STATE
OF PURE AND TOTAL PRESENCE

To THE JOYFUL ONE, (who has fully grasped) that
there is nothing that makes both (persons and
phenomena) what they are, who has acquired ever-
fresh awareness untainted by concepts, and primordial contact with the total field of events and
meanings;
To the quiet nature of everything, the supreme path in
which there is nothing to accept or reject;
To those who are one with all the Victorious Ones
(and possess) the ten powers, such as never turning
back;
To the very sameness of these three places of refuge, I
very confidently dedicate myself, without conceptualizing (this sameness). [1-4]

(The state of pure and total presence) is equally
praised by all Teachers who have been the light of
the world,
As the energy-pulse itself of the youthful Mañjuśri,
who is the energy-pulse of all reality;
As the mother of all the Joyful Ones, the one path of
all the Victorious Ones;
And as the basis of the ocean of ways, such as ethical
conduct, to overcome limitations. [5-8]

The specific benefit of having developed ongoing and
utmost pure and total presence is that,

When a perceptive person has made this noble pure
    and total presence real,

It is then what the Victorious Ones have spoken of as
    "primordial contact with the total field of events
    and meanings," most excellent of the three forms of
    primordial contact with reality.

It is also called the "eye of discernment" because of
    the excellence of its knowing capacity.

Nonconceptual, ever-fresh awareness, supreme and
    indestructible, is, moreover, also this very (state of
    pure and total presence).   [9–13]

Since all that can be said to be an aspect of the state of
    freedom of any of the Noble Ones

Comes about through the state of pure and total pres-
    ence reaching its fullness, these capacities arise from
    that.

Also, all those heroically committed to the state of
    pure and total presence, belonging to the deathless,
    great, noble lineage,

Could not come into being if this [pure and total pres-
    ence] did not exist. Therefore, it is the very path of
    supreme freedom.   [14–17]

How ought one, then, to cultivate this ever-present
    state of commitment to what is indestructible?

This path of all the great seers that is subtle and dif-
    ficult to understand, is beyond thought and no-
    thought.

It is divorced from verbal conventions in its being dif-
    ficult to point out and inquire into—

Thus it is not arrived at by words and is not in the
    realm of experiences of ordinary people and those
    apart from (the supreme, comprehensive approach
    to the teachings).   [18–21]

Although this is so, in this case one should look into
    the matter by means of the oral instructions of the
    masters and the definitive words of the Teacher.

From a logical basis in direct perception, etc., one
thinks about entities within the limited conceptions
of affirmation and denial;

But the very (thought) that follows in the wake of the
continual grasping of experience by thought, having affirmed something as a valid means of knowledge, is itself then contradicted by the mind.

Since the grasping of experience by thought does not
itself exist as something within our limiting conceptions, there is no limiting conception to be thought
about. If there is nothing to this (grasping by
thought), what valid means of knowledge can there
be?

Therefore, the conventional ways of inquiring into
things by worldly people are not necessary on this
yogic path.   [22-26]

Here, one should inquire into this path starting from
the characteristics that are the logical basis of our
limited conception: "an entity."

This reality, known as that which is present internally
and externally in the experience of all living beings,

Is not as it is seen and intended by the six forms of
apprehension, but is deceptive.

If that which is apprehended while intoxicated by
one's own grasping of experience by thought, was
valid,

It would then be reasonable to say that these (sentient
beings) would be free, just like those who have
overcome emotional conflicts, who think, "there
are no entities."

From the fact that these (sentient beings) are tormented by frustration and crushed by the enemy,
time, it is evident that they are deceived.

Otherwise, if that which is known through the sense
fields were a valid means of knowledge,

Then, this being so, who would have a need for the
noble path?

The path (of ordinary perception) is taught as the path
of freedom, although one is not freed through sense
perception.

Such perceptually based awareness, which does not
remove any frustration, is the birthplace of that
which muddies the stream of awareness.

Therefore, it has been stated by the Victorious Ones
that it is evident that what is perceived by sentient
beings is deceptive.   [27-37]

Then, how do these (appearances) make themselves
felt due to deception?

(One's potentiality for experience), which always and
everywhere tries to grasp experience through
thought, is automatically enfeebled by this grasping.

Since one's mental clarity, becoming deluded, has
come under the power of lack of awareness acting
as a conditioning factor,

The general forms and specific details of experiencing
appear as if existing-in-themselves, according to the
three phrases (of experience discussed below).

Through the accumulation of habituating tendencies
(engendered by) the various aspects of being caught
up in a situation, when the power of that habituation has grown,

The potential for experience itself appears in a manner
similar to that of the body and objects, as in the case
of (a meditation in which) bones appear everywhere.

The self, which is imagined by thought when it objec-
tifies the continuing stream of accumulating tendencies, does not exist.

By the power of being caught up in experiences, the
fundamental structuring of all experiencing has
been obscured and so this subtle (foundation) is not
seen. From this specific perceptions arise.   [38-45]

Through the power of the potential for experience
together with its continuing activity, one loses a
profound comprehension (of how things appear)
and, following in the wake of trying to grasp experience through thought,
Concepts of "self" and "entities" proliferate due to
this grasping, which is by nature unstable.
By not seeing this very subtle movement (of the fundamental structuring of all experience) that has
arisen possessing (the habituating tendencies), the
various philosophical views of the Hindus, such as
that of the self, arise and are held to be liberating.
Once the potential for experiencing has provided the
site for limitless actions, the duration of the habituating tendencies is endless and indeterminable,
While the conditions for the awakening and growth of
the habituating tendencies are various.
Although, through the maturation of (previously
accumulated) tendencies due to the appropriate
conditions, a human body appears,
When other conditions awaken other tendencies,
(there can be another form of life). Seeing the power of this process of change,
It is claimed that this is done by Śiva, etc. But that
path does not alleviate (suffering) or lead to liberation.
The enfeeblement of the yogic path as well as the
source of doubt arise from the lack of a profound
grasp of this subtle continuity [of the fundamental
structuring of all experience].   [46–55]

By imagining a self, one has completely obscured
(one's own existence) and been divorced from the
lineage of the Noble Ones.
By imagining entities, a variety of frustrations arises,
and so one will be reborn in the lower realms.
                                                   [56–57]

Since perception, moreover, seizes on different identi-
    fiable qualities out of the spectrum of conditioned
    events,
It appears as eightfold due to these specific activities,
    although it is not manifold in its essential function.
                                                    [58–59]

Therefore, in the first moment of experience, one's
    body and all configurations of events and meanings
    are present.
On account of thinking about and becoming obsessed
    with something, in a later (moment) that (thought)
    that has arisen (in accord with the earlier moment)
    makes itself felt.   [60–61]

Nothing exists for ordinary people and Noble Ones
    apart from the continuum of their own ex-
    periencing.
This variety (of experience) that exists for the six
    types of sentient beings (appears) through their
    own habitual mode of vision.
Since this continuum of experiencing is without any
    boundaries, (to call it) "one" is (also) without
    foundation.
Since that has no boundaries, all the limitless Buddha-
    fields are one's own body.
In that one's own body appears as the body of liv-
    ing beings and as limitless Buddha-fields, it is also
    difficult to postulate that the potential for experi-
    encing and the habituating tendencies are either one
    or diverse.   [62–67]

(One says), "all these (configurations of events and
    meanings) come about and disappear according to
    dependent origination." But, like a burnt seed,
    since a nonexistent (result) does not come about
    from a nonexistent (cause), cause and effect do not
    exist.

Being obsessed with entities, one's experiencing itself,
which discriminates each cause and effect, appears
as if it were cause and condition. [68–71A]

Since these two (cause and effect) do not exist, origination and cessation do not exist.
Since origination and cessation do not exist, self and
other do not exist. Since there is no transformation
and death, eternity and annihilation do not exist.
Therefore, it is evident that deceptive samsara as well
as nirvana do not exist. [71b–73]

The momentary site (i.e., the fundamental structuring) is never separate (from the habituating tendencies). They are really the same phenomenon and (if
one) does not exist, (the other) does not exist.
Since they are produced by trying to grasp experience
with thought, which is completely mistaken, the
habituating tendencies do not exist and,
Since there then does not exist a sphere of operation
(for the fundamental structuring), the fundamental
structuring of all experience as well as perceptual
and cognitive activities do not exist.
Since boundaries do not exist (in experience), an
objective support or a site (for its operation) do not
exist. How then can perceptual and cognitive activities arise?
Therefore, experiencing is beyond the limiting conceptions of existence and nonexistence, and is
neither a unity nor a plurality. [74–78]

Since the state of pure and total presence of the Joyful
One does not exist, it is a magical apparition of that
[state] that appears to those who are deluded. [79]

In the same way, although these pure forms of ever-
fresh awareness, (inseparable from) the total field of
events and meanings and the continuity of wholly

positive actions (connected with it), are imagined to
come about (in time) and be objectifiable,
Since there is no causal basis for vajra-like (ever-fresh
awareness), (our potential for experience, as causal
basis, and ever-fresh awareness, as result) are alike
regarding this similar condition (of nonexistence).
And,
Since these supreme forms of vajra-like (ever-fresh
awareness) that (thoroughly grasp) the total field of
events and meanings are without boundaries, they
are not momentary events.   [80–83]

Since the source of pure, positive qualities is nonexistent like a reflection, ever-fresh awareness that deals
with mundane matters does not exist.   [84]

Therefore, since what we define as "pure and total
presence" and "lack of pure and total presence" are
one in not existing, there is nothing to accept or
reject.
In this sense, then, the terms for the ultimate, such
as *nonexistence of origination and cessation, fundamental alikeness, nonduality, beyond thought,
openness, the total field of events and meanings,
beyond conventional designations and language*, are
all conventional designations. When the ultimate
does not exist, then the state of a pervasive lack of
clarity does not exist.
Saying that something ultimately is the case, is itself
the state of a pervasive lack of clarity.   [85–89]

One should not remain in a state wherein there is no
doubt, nor eleminate a state of doubt.
Since there is no meditator and no total field of events
and meanings (as object of meditation), there is
neither doubt nor genuine insight.   [90–91]

Since, if one inquires into our limiting conception
"entities," they are (found to be) nonexistent even
as regards their apparitional nature,

Then even this nonexistence, which is dependent
upon existence, is nonexistent. Also, the nonexistence of this nonexistence does not exist.
Since the limiting concepts do not exist, the middle
(between these) does not exist. One does not remain even in a "middle".   [92–94]

Just as the "Lotus-like Lord" of everything worldly
does not reject anything, (all things) are seen as
alike and present in utter sameness.
This very seeing as deceptive that which (is fundamentally not deceptive), is to be understood as
deception.
Even the teachings of the six (Hindu schools) and the
deeds of the Lord of limitations are not rejected and
regarded as negative.
Since even engaging in skillful action and discernment
do not exist, engaging in them is like the [activity]
of the Lord of limitations.
Having become proud through taking one's understanding as the best, superior to all, attachment and
aversion arise, from which arguments come about.
This is lack of awareness. The real point is not seen.
                                                 [95–100]

As long as there is the agitated movement of the mind,
there is the realm of the Lord of limitations. [This
practice of pure and total presence] is a subtle path,
in which one does not remain even in the states of
the absence of movement of thought or of nonmovement. This middle path in which there is no
deceptive appearance has been called the "primordial state of pure and total presence" by the
Awakened Ones.   [101–103]

Having eliminated holding on to form, identifiable
characteristics, and wishfulness, while cultivating
the three "gateways to freedom," is the activity of

the Lord of limitations. Form (itself) is open-
dimensional.
Eliminating the three paths of samsara while cultivating nirvana is also the activity of the Lord of limitations. This (kind of cultivation) is not the quiet
nature of everything. There is not any (samsara) eliminated or actual state (of nirvana) sought.
Nirvana and so forth, the status (reached) and realm
of vision of all the Noble Ones, do not exist apart
from this very path.   [104–108]

When (a thought) arises one does not eliminate it, nor
does one construct a support for the mind when no
(thought) arises.
(Even if) there stirs the slightest (thought) that is not
(the dimension of knowledge called) Mañjuśrī, this
itself is still that (dimension of knowledge). But one
does not try to remain in that.
Since one cannot obtain a foundation for meditation,
one will not obtain any result by meditation.
Grasping experience through thought, which is the
sphere of operation of our "mind," is itself the ultimate content of what is.
Since one is free from (seizing on) perceptible qualities, there does not exist anything that is better or
worse. This supreme path is to be cultivated.
Since neither do conditioned events arise (on their
own) nor do all configurations of events and meanings come about (dependently), all these are taken
beyond the realm of frustration and suffering.
When (one has thoroughly grasped that) there are no
"entities," everything then (arises) as the total field
of events and meanings—understanding this is the
supreme state of those who have overcome emotional conflicts.
Space is unobjectifiable and is a mere name. That
which is positive for an individual and that which is
negative, being indivisible, do not arise.   [109–116]

The mind is not engaged in seeking nor is it directed towards anything. One is free from knowing and not knowing.

There is neither picking out nor attending to (aids to meditation). Delight in acceptance and rejection are alike in not existing. Not objectifying (anything), and

Remaining with the (understanding of) this alikeness, there is no creation of duality; one is beyond the realm of speech; there is neither activity nor inactivity; there is no accumulation (of merit) or diminution (of faults), etc.   [117–119]

One's mind is not engaged in seeking anything. One is not disturbed by anything, knowing the fundamental alikeness (of everything); and

There is no fear of intoxication by objects or attachment to anything. One does not avoid nor dwell on (anything).

The ways of overcoming (limitations), the facets (of pure and total presence), the four forms of everfresh awareness of the alikeness (of everything), which are undisturbed (by negative conditions), are known in this (practice).

Cultivating the all-encompassing field of experience (is) this path; if one has cultivated otherwise, the transparent clarity (of the field) will not come about.   [120–123]

To really get (the meaning) through symbolic means is also "pure and total presence": so has the Teacher proclaimed.

(The symbolic means) are here the foundation for the activation and cultivation of pure and total presence itself.

Having made use of the three "symbolic encounters" that are indicative of (facets of the existence of an Awakened One), and made firm the three contemplations,

Primordial experience itself is activated in the "symbolic encounter with the ultimate content of what is." One should visualize and recite the heart-mantra (of the divinity that represents that).

[124-127]

By this "cultivation of the commitment to what is indestructible" all paths are unerringly cultivated.

If anything positive for the individual, whatever it may be, has not been taken up by the way of acting (symbolized by) Samantabhadrī,

Then the way of acting (symbolized by) Samantabhadra becomes the activity of the Lord of limitations—in which case it will reach its limit and be exhausted.

On the path that possesses this (primordial state of pure and total presence), even the activity of the Lord of limitations is said to be the activity of this pure and total presence.   [128-131]

Intense interest in the meaning of this, moreover, has been praised by the Victorious One as "great, pure and total presence."

By the mere activation of this source, the Awakened One has proclaimed, one will overcome the (limitations represented by) the host of the Lord of limitations, as well as the Śrāvakas, who are the object of veneration of the triple world and its rulers.

The greatest skillful action is this hidden activity of those committed to pure and total presence.

If this (state of pure and total presence) did not exist, the Victorious One could not make his appearance, and it would then be impossible that the three approaches to the teaching be taught.

In a mere instant, by the power of trusting confidence, moreover, one quickly becomes the youthful Mañjuśrī.

Also, while the supreme commitments of the su-

preme, comprehensive approach to the teachings
are kept and the hidden dimensions of existence entered, all commitments and ethical behavior are
protected and (those committed to pure and total
presence) greatly praised as a noble object for offer-
ings.

If the merit of the state of pure and total presence had
form, even the extent of space would be too small a
container for it, the Victorious Ones have equally
proclaimed.   [132–141]

Individual beings have been born, are being born, and
will be born in various forms of life, and thus have
come under the power of the stream of birth.

Through not understanding what the grasping of
experience through thought ultimately is, one is
deceived by this grasping. The stream of thought
continues, and so there is no (opportunity) to turn
away from deluded thought later on.

The illusory beings who are deceived by illusions such
as an illusory elephant, by those who are skilled in
the art of illusion, also lose their dreamlike happiness, just as when one is deceived by a dream (into
thinking it is real). Since those who have come
under the power of dreams

Reject this path and look to other paths that are
extreme, and teach (that) as what they call the
"unerring path," they are fit for a compassionate
(response). They are like those who say stone is
gold. The compassion of the compassionate ones
(is spontaneous), their minds being conditioned by
commiseration.

These sentient beings who suffer because of the temporal circumstances and do not exercise (discernment) during these last 500 years of the teaching,

Have difficulty understanding the pure teaching, and
going by mere words, do not (understand it) properly.

The various points of view (that result) are confirmed
according to each one's own capacity, etc. One is
stirred up by this river of misunderstanding and
separated from the yogic ambrosia that is the vital
essence of the teaching.   [142-151]
Therefore, although this noble hidden dimension of
primordial experiencing, the excellent path taught
by the Victorious Ones,
Is the extra-ordinary sphere of operation of the primordial experience of all the Victorious Ones,
I have validated (it for myself) by virtue of (long)
experience and noncontradictory valid means of
knowledge.
By composing this (work) on the excellent path of
nonduality for the sake of sentient beings,
May, in a single moment, in all the places of birth of
sentient beings,
Obstacles decrease and this primordial experience of
all the Victorious Ones spread.   [152-157]

The Commentary

CULTIVATING THE PRIMORDIAL STATE OF PURE AND TOTAL
PRESENCE DISCUSSED UNDER TWELVE HEADINGS

HOMAGE TO THE THREE JEWELS!

Cultivating the Primordial State of Pure and Total Presence
can be discussed under twelve headings:

1. Gesture of respect
2. Why (the primordial state) should be fully grasped
3. What should be fully grasped
4. How it can be fully grasped
5. What has to be inquired into to fully grasp (the primordial state)
6. Pointing out the real meaning[1] (grasped) after inquiring into (the above)
7. Putting the real meaning into practice
8. Special methods taught for fully grasping the real meaning
9. Pointing out that without taking hold of the primordial state of pure and total presence, freedom will not be obtained and positive qualities will come to an end
10. Pointing out that even the arousal of mere intense interest (in the primordial state) leads to many abilities
11. Pointing out that those who have gone wrong are the object of compassion
12. Dedication for (the sake of creating) a foundation of positive qualities

1. The gesture of respect is made three times, once to the Awakened One, once to the Teaching, and once to the Community. The teacher Mañjuśrīmitra begins his text with this gesture, shown in the first verse, in order to avoid and finally overcome obstacles. The gesture of respect to the Awakened One is shown by the line,

> To the Joyful One, (who has fully grasped) that there is nothing that makes both (persons and phenomena) what they are, who has acquired ever-fresh awareness untainted by concepts, and primordial contact with the total field of events and meanings;   [1]

The full grasp, without mistakes, that there is nothing that makes both persons and phenomena what they are, is itself the ever-fresh awareness of the Joyful One, untainted by concepts. Obtaining this fresh awareness, one acquires its domain, the total field of events and meanings, as well as the primordial contact inseparable from that domain.

The gesture of respect to the Teaching is,

> To the quiet nature of everything, the supreme path in which there is nothing to accept or reject;   [2]

In the actual condition of all that which muddies the stream of awareness, as well as its purification, the (proliferation) of all such characterizations by the discursive mind ceases. In this there are no positive qualities to acquire and no faults to remove. (This) absence of acceptance and rejection is supreme among paths of freedom.

The gesture of respect to the Community is

> To those who are one with all the Victorious Ones (and possess) the ten powers, such as never turning back;   [3]

Those who are heroically committed to pure and total presence, residing on the ten spiritual levels, do not fall back into samsara upon (attaining) the first level, do not fall back into (seizing on) identifiable characteristics upon (attaining) the eighth, etc.[2] (They possess) the powers over life, action, material goods, etc.[3] Those who obtain these ten powers are one with all the Victorious Ones by virtue of their unity with the full grasp of the total field of events and meanings.

> To the very sameness of these three places of refuge, I very
> confidently dedicate myself, without conceptualizing
> (this sameness). [4]

The place of refuge is the three jewels. The ultimate content of what is, is the unerring path. This is what is to be known; the Awakened Ones and those heroically committed to Awakening are those who know this. Since (here) there is what is called the "nondistinction between knowing and what is known," (one speaks of) "fundamental alikeness"; and since ultimately there is nonduality, (one also speaks of) "fundamental alikeness." In this regard, through a dedication that adheres to, with certainty, reality as it is, and through the pure confidence of a mind that is not attached to its ways of characterizing things, the gesture of respect is made.

2. If one asks, why should the primordial state of pure and total presence be fully grasped?, the answer is: on account of its great benefit. This benefit, further, has three aspects: (a) its beneficial existence as the motivating cause (of freedom); (b) its benefit as the specific goal that is fully grasped; and (c) pointing out that it is the supreme basis, as well as path, of all the fruits of freedom.

a. Of these, the beneficial existence as motivating cause is spoken of as follows:

> (The primordial state) is equally praised by all Teachers
> who have been the light of the world, [5]

and so forth. All teachers of gods and men, who have become the light of ever-fresh awareness that clears away the inner and outer darkness of the world, equally and similarly praise the primordial state of pure and total presence as being of great benefit. If one asks how they praise it, the answer is:

> As the energy-pulse itself of the youthful Mañjuśrī, who is
> the energy-pulse of all reality; [6]

In this case, whether or not "those who have come through" visit (our reality), the ultimate content of what is, the energy-pulse of all that is, present since the very beginning, is what we call the "youthful Mañjuśrī." Why is he called "gentle," etc.?⁴ He is gentle because there is no irritation, and realizing this, one becomes Lord of all beings. "Youthful" has the meaning of pure, since he is not tainted by faults and impurities. "Energy-pulse" is mentioned above since it is the energy-pulse of all reality. "Mañjuśrī" is the unerring thorough comprehension that is the defining characteristic of the primordial state of pure and total presence, since it is the birthplace of all Awakened Ones.

> As the mother of all the Joyful Ones, the one path of all the
> Victorious Ones;   [7]

is stated because, if one has not understood this path, one won't become an Awakened One by another path.

> And as the basis of the ocean of ways, such as ethical con-
> duct, to overcome (limitations).   [8]

If one has not taken hold of the ten ways of overcoming (limitations), such as ethical conduct, etc., as well as other wholesome activities, with this primordial state, then the accumulation (of merit) that leads to the state of an Awakened One has not been accomplished. Thus, it is also shown that (the primordial state) is the basis of all the merits accumulated for the sake of reaching the state of an Awakened One.

  b. Pointing out the distinguishing superiority (of the primordial state) also at the time of the goal, i.e., when it is made really so, is as follows:

> The specific benefit of having developed ongoing and
> utmost pure and total presence is that,   [9]

When one has cultivated unerringly, in actuality and in its ongoingness, the primordial state of pure and total presence that is pure delight, so that it is really so, what are the specific abilities which are obtained? The answer is:

When a perceptive person has made this noble pure and
total presence real,
It is then what the Victorious Ones have spoken of as "primordial contact with the total field of events and meanings," most excellent of the three forms of primordial
contact with reality. [10-11]

When those who possess a discerning mind make this primordial experience of pure and total presence really so, the primordial state is then called "primordial contact with the total
field of events and meanings," which is the most excellent
among the three forms of primordial contact, such as "primordial contact with total richness and all its satisfactions."[5]
Since this primordial state of pure and total presence, which is
the basis of all that is positive and of all capacities, is primordial contact with the total field of events and meanings, it is
most excellent.

It is also called the "eye of discernment" because of the
excellence of its knowing capacity. [12]

Among all the means of knowing, the most noble is the "eye
of discernment." Why? Since among all objects of knowledge, the ultimate content of what is, which is the energy-
pulse of all that is, is the most worthy, so also the means of
knowing that thoroughly grasps this is called "worthy."
Also, among the five types of "eyes"[6] such as the physical eye
and the "eye of the gods," the "eye of discernment," which
by definition makes the primordial state of pure and total
presence a reality, is supreme.

Nonconceptual, ever-fresh awareness, supreme and indestructible, is, moreover, also this very (state of pure and
total presence). [13]

A vajra is hard and can cut (anything). It is (called) "hard,"
because it is not broken by any contrary substance; and since
it eliminates, i.e., cuts through, all obscuring elements, it is
referred to as ever-fresh awareness. Since it is the pinnacle,
i.e., supreme, among the four forms of ever-fresh awareness,[7]

such as the discriminating ever-fresh awareness, the all-accomplishing ever-fresh awareness, etc., it is (called) non-conceptual ever-fresh awareness. Moreover, the making real of the primordial state of pure and total presence is just this.

c. Pointing out (this primordial state) as the supreme basis, as well as path, of all the fruits of freedom, is shown by the following:

> Since all that can be said to be an aspect of the state of
> freedom of any of the Noble Ones   [14]

Also, all of that which is shown to be, and reported as, the capacities that result from freedom from the three realms, such as those of the Śrāvakas and Pratyekabuddhas,

> Comes about through the state of pure and total presence
> reaching its fullness, these capacities arise from that.
>   [15]

While from the thorough grasp and fulfillment of the state of pure and total presence arises the fulfillment of one's capacities, even if one thoroughly grasps this primordial state at a low or middling level (of understanding), corresponding capacities will also arise and be obtained. Those who do not thoroughly grasp the state of pure and total presence at all, do not obtain even a minimal freedom. Therefore, since this is both the basis of all freedom and the path which accomplishes the excellent result, it is supreme among paths of freedom. If one asks why, the answer is:

> Also, all of those heroically committed to the state of pure
> and total presence, belonging to the deathless, great, no-
> ble lineage,   [16]

Since the supreme comprehensive approach is the great goal among all the noble lineages of Śrāvakas, etc., it is called the "great lineage." Those who are intent on the great, unsurpassed state of pure and total presence are called "those who are heroically committed to pure and total presence." Even all those

> Could not come into being if this (pure and total presence)
> did not exist. Therefore, it is the very path of supreme
> freedom.   [17]

If this state of pure and total presence did not exist, then,
since there could not be those who are heroically committed
to it, this state is most excellent among all paths to freedom.
3. If one asks, what should be fully grasped, the answer is:
the primordial state of pure and total presence. Further, (the
author) points out that it is not an object of inquiry, since it is
beyond words and thought:

> How ought one, then, to cultivate this ever-present state of
> commitment to what is indestructible?   [18]

The great benefit spoken of above is not destroyed anywhere
or at any time. Since the thorough grasp of this cuts through
the net of obscuring elements (in a person), it is (called)
"vajra."[8] As regards the unerring felt knowledge of the ultimate content of our potential for experience, it is called the
"state of commitment to what is indestructible" and "primordial state of pure and total presence." Due to an accidental
loss of this felt knowledge, which is characteristic of our
potential for experience, all that which muddies the stream of
awareness is pervasively present. When "the state of commitment to what is indestructible," the actual condition of our
potential for experience, is thoroughly grasped without mistake, the excellence of the fruit of freedom is present. So, by
what means ought one unerringly to cultivate (this)? The
answer to this question is:

> This path of all the great seers that is subtle and difficult to
> understand, is beyond thought and no-thought.   [19]

Since it is not understood by those of undeveloped intellect or
by those who are attached to their intellect, it is subtle and
difficult to know. Thus, this path of the Awakened One, the
great seer, which has been entered upon or is (now) at first
entered upon by myself and others, is not an object of
thought. Yet, since it is also not an object (called) "no-

thought," it is beyond both thought and no-thought. Therefore,

> It is divorced from verbal conventions in its being difficult
> to point out and inquire into—   [20]

While it is difficult for the mind to inquire into (this path) and
also difficult to point it out by words, what is being referred
to can be shown by words. Since the words are not what is
referred to, (this path) is beyond conventional designations.

> Thus it is not arrived at by words and is not in the realm of
> experience of ordinary people and those apart from (the
> supreme, comprehensive approach to the teachings).
>   [21]

Since what is referred to is beyond verbal conventions, it is
not arrived at by words. It is not an object for ordinary people and those apart from the supreme, comprehensive
approach, such as the Śrāvakas. Yet, the means for understanding and knowing it do exist.

4. If the means for fully grasping (this primordial state)
exist, how then can it be fully grasped? Since mistakenly trying to grasp experience through thought is not a valid means
of knowledge,[9] (the author) points out what is to be fully
grasped through thinking things through logically, according
to the characteristics of things as they really are and to the
testimony of scholars and Noble Ones, as follows:

> Although this is so, in this case one should look into the
> matter by means of the oral instructions of the masters
> and the definitive words of the Teacher.   [22]

In this case, one should look into this *Cultivating the Primordial State of Pure and Total Presence* in order not to err regarding that very (experience); into the oral instructions that
(come from) the unerring experience of thorough comprehension of the wise masters; and into the teachings that give the
real meaning, although there have been many things taught by
the Teacher (the Awakened One).

Pointing out that mistakenly grasping experience through thought is not a valid means of knowledge, is as follows:

> From a logical basis in direct perception, etc., one thinks
> about entities within the limited conception of affirma-
> tion and denial;   [23]

From a starting point that is reasonable, such as perception, sound thinking, etc., one assigns entities either to the category of that which muddies the stream of awareness, or that which clarifies the stream of awareness. A logical analysis asks: will something finally be found to be existent or nonexistent (according to its categories)?

> But the very (thought) that follows in the wake of the con-
> tinual grasping of experience by thought, having affirmed
> something as a valid means of knowledge, is itself then
> contradicted by the mind.   [24]

This very analysis mentioned above, following the stream of the mistaken grasping of experience through thought, and taking as a valid object of knowledge what is wrongly seen through this mistaken grasping, is (itself) either accepted or rejected by the mind that is mistaken. For example, when one sees a rope as a snake, why, since one sees (the snake) directly, does one say that there is no snake? Because taking one's own error as a valid, direct perception is not a valid means of knowledge. If one further asks why, the answer is:

> Since the grasping of experience by thought does not itself
> exist as something within our limiting conceptions, there
> is no limiting conception to be thought about. If there is
> nothing to this (grasping by thought), what valid means
> of knowledge can there be?   [25]

Since, ultimately, the mind itself that thinks is not to be found at all, how can there exist the activity of this (mind)? Therefore, there is no limiting conception (that the mind uses to think) to be thought about. If, in essence, there is no activity whatsoever, what valid means of knowledge can be asserted?

Therefore, the conventional ways of inquiring into things
by worldly people are not necessary on this yogic path.

[26]

When our relative existence has come under the power of the
deceptiveness of how things appear[10] due to the impossibility
of a (truly) valid means of knowledge, still, conventional
means of inquiry by worldly people validly exist. However,
in reality, at this stage of the yogic path of linking up (to
direct insight into reality),[11] the mistaken conventions of the
world are not necessary.

5. What has to be inquired into to fully grasp (this primordial state) has two aspects: (a) an inquiry into that which
muddies the stream of awareness, and (b) an inquiry into that
which is the clarification (of the stream of awareness).

a. An inquiry into that which muddies the stream of awareness also has two aspects: (i) an inquiry into just what is
meant by "that which muddies the stream of awareness," and
(ii) an inquiry into the deceptiveness of how things appear.

a.i. An inquiry into just what is meant by "that which muddies the stream of awareness" is pointed out in the following:

> Here, one should inquire into this path starting from the
> characteristics that are the logical basis of our limited
> conception: "an entity."   [27]

The reason for inquiring into the limits within which we
establish our conception of an "entity," is that, since one
establishes the unerring path (to freedom) through inquiring
into the defining characteristics of entities themselves, then in
this case of seeking the ultimate path, one should inquire like-
wise. For example, water's defining characteristic of coolness
is shown by what is characteristic of water's own essence.
Also, in a canonical text it states: "To those with a thinking
mind, demonstrate the characteristics of entities." Since the
knowledge and thorough grasp, just as they are, of the entities
which make up that which muddies the stream of awareness
as well as its clarification, is the unerring path, it is necessary

to seek the path through inquiring into the defining characteristics of entities.

> This reality, known as that which is present internally and
>   externally in the experience of all living beings,   [28]

This reality, which is known as the six outer objects and the
six internal knowing capacities, which (both) appear to be
objects, and are known by the mind of sentient beings,

> Is not as it is seen and intended by the six forms of
>   apprehension, but is deceptive.   [29]

The six modes of awareness[12] make a delimited object out of
seeing and hearing, etc. But whatever appears so, does not so
exist, since it is deceptive.

> If that which is apprehended while intoxicated by one's
>   own grasping of experience by thought, was valid,   [30]

If that which is delusively seen by a person intoxicated with
grasping after experience through thought, which is itself a
lack of awareness, were true, then

> It would then be reasonable to say that these (sentient
>   beings) would be free, just like those who have overcome
>   emotional conflicts, who think, "there are no entities."
>   [31]

Although those who have overcome emotional conflicts, and
sentient beings, are different; since, (in this case), there would
be no distinction in their seeing of what is true, it would stand
to reason that both would obtain the goal of freedom.

> From the fact that these (sentient beings) are tormented by
>   frustration and crushed by the enemy, time, it is evident
>   that they are deceived.   [32]

These sentient beings are tormented by the three and the eight
frustrations,[13] and crushed by the enemy, time, as in illness
and death. Therefore, it is evident that the ways of seeing of
sentient beings are deceived.

> Otherwise, if that which is known through the sense fields
> were a valid means of knowledge,   [33]

(That which is known) is deceptive; furthermore, if it were
not deceptive and that which is known through the twelve
bases of our field of awareness[14] were a valid means of knowledge,

> Then, this being so, who would have a need for the noble
> path?   [34]

(This is so), since the noble path would exist in its own right
in sentient beings.

> The path (of ordinary perception) is taught as the path of
> freedom, although one is not freed through sense percep-
> tion.
>   [35]

What sentient beings see due to deception is claimed as the
path to freedom, but one is not freed from the frustration of
samsara by perception based on the physical sense organs.
Why? As to the perceptions of various perceptible qualities
by sentient beings,

> Such perceptually based awareness, which does not remove
> any frustration, is the birthplace of that which muddies
> the stream of awareness.   [36]

How can (perception) eliminate frustration and suffering,
since it is their birthplace?

> Therefore, it has been stated by the Victorious Ones that it
> is evident that what is perceived by sentient beings is de-
> ceptive.   [37]

Thus, that which is perceived by sentient beings is, according
to reason, manifestly deceptive; also according to the authoritative words of the Awakened One it is said to be deceptive.

a.ii. The second part of the inquiry into that which muddies
the stream of awareness has nine sections, dealing with the
deceptiveness of how things appear:

A. What appears

B. Why it appears

C. How the deceptiveness of how things appear obstructs (the path)

D. What defines perception, which is the basis of all appearance

E. How that which is to appear becomes present

F. Nothing need be added or gotten, because everything is already included within our potential for experience, which is itself what is present (when anything presents itself).

G. An answer to the question: If everything is our emerging potential for experience, why do some things and happenings appear to originate from independent conditions?

H. That which appears, things and happenings, is not to be found at all (if inquired into).

I. Even our potential for experience, from which all appearance arises, is not to be found at all (if inquired into).

A. As to the first, if one asks, what appears?, in answer it is pointed out that our potential for experience itself, by virtue of deception, is what is present as various perceptible qualities.

> Then, how do these (appearances) make themselves felt due to deception? [38]

Since it is evident that (what appears) is deceptive, then how do these appearances come about for these sentient beings through deception? The answer is:

> (One's potentiality for experience), which always and everywhere tries to grasp experience through thought, is automatically enfeebled by this grasping. [39]

The potential for experience of sentient beings naturally tries, always and everywhere, to grasp experience through thought. Through this grasping, which is deceived and inauthentic, one has, without doing anything, lost sight of the truth.

> Since one's mental clarity, becoming deluded, has come
> under the power of lack of awareness acting as a con-
> ditioning factor,   [40]

Since one does not see the truth, one's mental clarity becomes
deluded; and since one does not then possess the ability to see
the truth, one comes under the power of ignorance of the
flash of knowing that gives awareness its (illumining) quality.

> The general forms and specific details of experiencing
> appear as if existing-in-themselves, according to the three
> phases (of experience discussed below).   [41]

The general form of experience consists of the eight modes of
awareness,[15] from which arise the specific details of experience. These details are the fifty-one aspects of being caught up
in experiencing.[16] Our potential for experience appears as if
existing objectively in-itself, according to the three phases
discussed below.[17]

> Through the accumulation of habituating tendencies (en-
> gendered by) the various aspects of being caught up in a
> situation, when the power of that habituation has grown,
>   [42]

By becoming habituated to the accumulated tendencies (engendered by) the various aspects of being caught up in positive and negative actions, these previously acquired tendencies mature and spread. When they possess the power of
sending forth their fruit,

> The potential for experience itself appears in a manner simi-
> lar to that of the body and objects, as in the case of (a
> meditation in which) bones appear everywhere.   [43]

The potential for experience itself appears in a manner similar
to that of the body internally and objects externally. For
example, when meditating on "impurity," one meditates on
the whole world as full of bones;[18] meditating thus for a long
time, when the power (of the practice) has grown and the
whole world seems full of bones, it is one's own potential for

experience that appears as bones. Of the three phases, the above points out the first. The second is:

> The self, which is imagined by thought when it objectifies the continuing stream of accumulating tendencies, does not exist. [44]

The arising of the conception that the evanescent stream of the fundamental structuring of all experience, together with the habituating tendencies, is a self, is nothing apart from the thinking mind. Therefore, the self, which is imagined through the power of the thought, "I," does not exist. For example, it is like the case in which, although one has taken a multi-colored rope to be a snake, apart from the mere thought of a snake there does not exist in the rope the characteristic of being a snake. The third phase is:

> By the power of being caught up in situations, the fundamental structuring of all experiencing has been obscured and so this subtle (foundation) is not seen. From this specific perceptions arise. [45]

The subtle fundamental structuring of all experience has been obscured by the gross appearance of the various aspects of being caught up in a situation. From not seeing this (process), perceptions and acts of knowing appear like (a mirage). For example, it is just as in the case of the arising of the thought of water when one doesn't know that it is a mirage.

B. Of this ninefold division, the second is why (the deceptiveness of how things appear) makes itself felt. The answer is: on account of not seeing how the fundamental structuring of all experience actually is. It is just as in the example of the arising of the erroneous (perception) of a snake on account of not seeing how the rope (which is the basis of this error) actually is.

> Through the power of the potential for experience together with its continuing activity, one loses a profound comprehension (of how things appear), and, following in the wake of trying to grasp experience through thought, [46]

One does not understand that how things appear in their variety is due to the power of the fundamental structuring of all experience, together with the habituating tendencies. Therefore, following in the wake of the mistaken grasping after experience through thought, due to the fact that all appearances (now) have an existence of their own,

> Concepts of "self" and "entities" proliferate due to this
> grasping, which is by nature unstable.   [47]

In the wake of this mistake, the concepts of "self," which is accidentally imagined by this grasping of experience by thought and is the motivating cause of samsara and the fall into the three realms of existence; as well as that of "entities," internal and external, proliferate.

> By not seeing this very subtle movement (of the fun-
> damental structuring of all experience) that has arisen
> possessing (the habituating tendencies), the various phi-
> losophical views of the Hindus, such as that of the self,
> arise and are held to be liberating.   [48–49]

It can be demonstrated that, through not seeing the neck-lacelike fundamental structuring of all experience, the many forms of Hinduistic philosophy arise.[19] If one asks why they arise, the answer (follows in the next verses):

> Once the potential for experience has provided the site for
> limitless actions, the duration of the habituating tenden-
> cies is endless and indeterminable,   [50]

The fundamental structuring of all experience, which is called our "potential for experience," is the site for the limitless habituating tendencies connected with good and evil actions. Since the habituating tendencies present in the fundamental structuring are limitless, there is no way to be certain and say that these habituating tendencies are not present (at any time when the fundamental structuring exists).

> While the conditions for the awakening and growth of the
> habituating tendencies are various.   [51]

The habituating tendencies remain "in" the fundamental structuring. Variously, through positive conditions the tendency towards birth in the higher realms of existence arises; while through negative conditions and the muddying of the stream of awareness, the tendency towards birth in the lower realms of existence arises.

> Although, through the maturation of (previously accumulated) tendencies due to the appropriate conditions, a human body appears, [52]

Through the maturation and awakening of tendencies that were present previously in the process of fundamental structuring and that make for human birth in this life, a human body is obtained and manifests itself.

> When other conditions awaken other tendencies, (there can be another form of life). Seeing the power of this process of change, [53]

When the tendencies, previously present in the fundamental structuring process that are the motivating cause of birth as a god mature and awaken due to the conditions for birth as a god, i.e., one other than human, seeing this change from human into god,

> It is claimed that this is done by Śiva, etc. But that path does not alleviate (suffering) or lead to liberation. [54]

The change of birth from man to god is seen by worldly supernormal perception;[20] yet through not understanding that this birth as a god (comes about) only through its own causes and conditions, one thinks that this is accomplished by a creator such as Śiva, and one claims that the path to freedom is based on the creator.[21] But (in this case), since frustration and suffering are not alleviated, one will not even be freed from the faults of the three realms of existence.

> The enfeeblement of the yogic path as well as the source of doubt arise from the lack of a profound grasp of this subtle continuity (of the fundamental structuring of all experience). [55]

One becomes diverted from the yogic path to reality; the cause of doubt and enfeeblement (on the path) also are born through not understanding this subtle movement of the fundamental structuring of all experience. For example, it is as in the case of one who doesn't really know a rope as it is and takes it to be a snake, or is in doubt, thinking, "Is it a snake or not?"

Then, when these various forms of experience arise through deception, what obstacle is there, one might ask?

c. Pointing out that the deceptiveness of how things appear is an obstacle: this is the third of the ninefold division.

> By imagining a self, one has completely obscured (one's own existence) and been divorced from the lineage of the Noble Ones.   [56]

Since those who belong to the lineage of the Noble Ones do not have the concept of self, by imagining a self in regard to what is not a self, there is the obstacle of not obtaining the goal (freedom) and of being divorced from the lineage of the Noble Ones.

> By imagining entities, a variety of frustrations arises, and so one will be reborn in the lower realms.   [57]

Through imagining a variety of entities one enters into various actions. By various actions various frustrations also will be experienced, and one will be reborn in the three lower realms through this unwholesome activity.

D. The fourth of the ninefold division is how to define perception, the basis of all appearance.

> Since perception, moreover, seizes on different identifiable qualities out of the spectrum of conditioned events,
>
>   [58]

By seizing on, through perception, the different identifiable characteristics of conditioned events, such as sound and form,

> It appears as eightfold due to these specific activities, although it is not manifold in its essential function.
>
>   [59]

Since there exist the eight modes of perceiving the identifiable characteristics of conditioned events, such as seeing form and hearing sound, awareness is taken as eightfold.[22] However, there are not multiple types (of awareness), since they all have the typical function of knowing and being aware.

E. The fifth of the ninefold division is: how is the variety of what is to appear (present) in the fundamental structuring process?

> Therefore, in the first moment of experience, one's body
> and all configurations of events and meanings are pres-
> ent.   [60]

As shown above, since there do not (actually) exist different (forms of) the potential for experience, in only one moment of this potential, i.e., the fundamental structuring of all experience, the body together with its sensory organs, as well as all other entities, are present. If one asks: why are there appearances homogeneous with the previous ones in the subsequent moments of experiencing, the answer is,

> On account of thinking about and becoming obsessed with
> something, in a later (moment) that (thought) that has
> arisen (in accord with the earlier moment) makes itself
> felt.   [61]

(The author) points out that something appears (in some way) by virtue of attachment to and obsession with it; therefore, just as one became obsessed thinking about something previous, later there arises thus an appearance in accord with (the former).[23]

F. The sixth of the ninefold division is to point out that nothing need be gotten, because everything is included within our potential for experience, which is the basis of appearance.

> Nothing exists for ordinary people and Noble Ones apart
> from the continuum of their own experiencing.   [62]

As explained above, all configurations of events and meanings, without exception, are present in the first moment of experiencing.

> This variety (of experience) that exists for the six types of
> sentient beings (appears) through their own habitual
> mode of vision.   [63]

The six types of sentient beings, such as men and gods, are
(actually) a single type appearing variously. These (six) are
moreover, appearances through the power of a habitual mode
of vision that they have become acquainted with and accustomed to, but which has no beginning in time. If one asks:
how is there nonduality due to the fact that all (appearance) is
(not other than) oneself? The answer is:

> Since this continuum of experiencing is without any
> boundaries, (to call it) "one" is (also) without founda-
> tion.   [64]

All of that which muddies the stream of awareness, as well as
its clarification, are one's own potential for experience. In this
momentary flow of experiencing there cannot be shown a
single thing, saying "this is like this," regarding directions
such as above and below, east and west, or limits such as
existence and nonexistence. Therefore, even the oneness (of
experience) cannot be pointed out.

> Since that has no boundaries, all the limitless Buddha-fields
> are one's own body.   [65]

If (even) a single boundary or division existed (in the potential
for experience), its "oneness" could not be demonstrated; this
is even more so in the case of a thing. If one then says that (the
potential for experience) is just like the sky, which is not a
thing (and hence unitary), we also reply that one can't make
this into a "oneness," since in the empty sky there are various
directions of center and periphery, as well as directions such
as east and west. Since ultimately there is no partiality whatsoever in the continuum of experience, it is indivisible into
parts. Since it is one in its not being able to be made into an
object, it actually is the pure and impure Buddha-fields.[24]

> In that one's own body appears as the body of living beings
> and as limitless Buddha-fields, it is also difficult to postu-

> late that the potential for experiencing and the habituat-
> ing tendencies are either one or diverse.   [66–67]

Thus, since everything is one's own dimension, and one's own dimension is oneself, and one's own dimension is every-thing, from the beginning there is no obtaining of what has not been obtained previously. It is difficult also to imagine that the potentiality for experience and habituating tendencies are either one or diverse; they are neither one nor many. For example, it is impossible to say whether color and shape are one or diverse.

G. The seventh of the ninefold division is the question: if everything is our potential for experience, why do things appear to arise from independent causes and conditions?

> (One says), "all these (configurations of events and mean-
> ings) come about and disappear according to dependent
> originations." But, like a burnt seed, since a nonexistent
> (result) does not come about from a nonexistent (cause),
> cause and effect do not exist.   [68–69]

It is said that all configurations of events and meanings come about as a result of depending on a cause; while if there is no basis existing, they cease. For example, as in the case of a burnt seed that does not give rise to a fruit, all configurations of events and meanings are not, in actuality, to be found. Since from a nonexistent cause a nonexistent result does not arise, there is no saying, "this is the cause and this is the effect." Well, then, why does it seem to all sentient beings that a result comes about based on a cause?

> Being obsessed with entities, one's experiencing itself,
> which discriminates each cause and effect, appears as if it
> were cause and condition.   [70–71a]

Since beginningless time it is just our potential for experience itself that thinks of and is obsessed with the reality of the causation of entities, and appears as if it were cause and effect. How is it possible that our potentiality for experience mani-fests itself from a nonexistent cause and effect? In a dream, for example, from the cause of having drunk beer, there appears the result of intoxication, and from cultivating a field, a harvest seems to come about. In the same way, while cause and effect do not exist entitatively, since beginningless time they appear as in a dream by virtue of the discrimination of cause and effect.

H. The eighth of the ninefold division is to point out that that which appears, things and happenings, is not to be found at all (if inquired into).

> Since these two (cause and effect) do not exist, origination
> and cessation do not exist.   [71b]

Since these two, cause and effect, do not exist, the arising of an effect dependent on a cause does not exist. If (something) is not produced, what basis for its cessation is there? Cessation also does not exist.

> Since origination and cessation do not exist, self and other
> do not exist. Since there is no transformation and death,
> eternity and annihilation do not exist.   [72]

If there is no origination and no cessation, what is "self," what is "other"? If there is no self and other, who dies, who is transformed? Thus, since there is no death, there is no annihilation. Since there is no transformation, there is no permanence.

> Therefore, it is evident that deceptive samsara as well as
> nirvana do not exist.   [73]

Birth and death, eternalism and nihilism, etc. do not exist. Therefore, since it follows that deception and samsara also do not exist, it is evident that nirvana, which is based on there being samsara, also does not exist.

I. The last of the ninefold division is to point out that even our potential for experience itself, which is the basis of appearance, is not to be found (if inquired into):

> The momentary site (i.e., the fundamental structuring) is
> never separate (from the habituating tendencies). They

> are really the same phenomenon and (if one) does not
> exist, (the other) does not exist.   [74]

The momentary fundamental structuring process that is the
site for the habituating tendencies, and the habituating tendencies themselves, are never separate. If the fundamental
structuring of all experience does not exist, the habituating
tendencies cannot exist. For example, if color didn't exist,
shape couldn't exist. If shape were nonexistent, color couldn't
exist. They are the same in that if one exists, then both exist;
or if one doesn't exist, then both don't exist. The habituating
tendencies not existing, the fundamental structuring of all experience also does not exist. Why?

> Since they are produced by trying to grasp experience with
>   thought, which is completely mistaken, the habituating
>   tendencies do not exist and,   [75]

Since they are produced by the mistaken grasping after experience through thought, it is not possible that the habituating tendencies can be said to exist. If these habituating tendencies do not exist,

> Since there then does not exist a sphere of operation (for
>   the fundamental structuring), the fundamental structur-
>   ing of all experience as well as perceptual and cognitive
>   activities do not exist.   [76]

The sphere of operation of the fundamental structuring process is the habituating tendencies. Since the habituating tendencies do not exist, their sphere of operation does not exist.
Since cognitive activity cannot come about if it has no object,
the fundamental structuring, which is dependent on its sphere
of operation, also does not exist. Also, all cognitive operations (based on the fundamental structuring) are just nonexistent.

> Since boundaries do not exist (in experience), an objective
>   support or a site (for its operation) do not exist. How
>   then can perceptual and cognitive activities arise?   [77]

Since it was shown above that any boundaries (in the potential for experience) are not to be found, the habituating tendencies that are an object for the mind, as well as the fundamental structuring of all experience that is the site (of their operation), do not exist. Then how can cognitive operations that are based on this arise?

> Therefore, experiencing is beyond the limiting conceptions
>   of existence and nonexistence, and is neither a unity nor a
>   plurality.   [78]

The general form and specific details of experiencing are nothing whatsoever. Therefore, in being beyond existence and nonexistence, they can't be "one" or "many."

b. The inquiry into that which is the clarification (of the stream of awareness) also has two aspects: (i) Pointing out that this state of clarification makes itself felt within deception itself; and (ii) pointing out that this very appearance also is not to be found (if inquired into).

b.i. Pointing out how the state of clarification makes itself felt within the state of deception is as follows:

> Since the state of pure and total presence of the Joyful One
>   does not exist, it is a magical apparition of that (state)
>   that appears to those who are deluded.   [79]

Since even the awakened state of the Joyful One ultimately is not to be found, it is evident that a magical display of this, like an apparition, appears in this case to those who are deluded. Thus, the *Diamond Sūtra* states:[25]

> Those who see me as form, those who know me as sound,
> Have entered the wrong path—these beings do not see me.
> The Awakened Ones see the ultimate content of what is.
>   The real guides (of living beings) are their primordial
>   contact with the total field of events and meanings. [The
>   ultimate content of what is not an object of knowledge,
>   therefore it cannot be perceived.]

b.ii. Also, pointing out that the appearance of the state of clarification is not to be found, has two aspects: (A) pointing out that nonconceptual ever-fresh awareness is not to be found; and (B) pointing out that a pure, though worldly, ever-fresh awareness is not to be found.

A. How is it that nonconceptual ever-fresh awareness is not to be found (if inquired into)?

> In the same way, although these pure forms of ever-fresh awareness, [inseparable from] the total field of events and meanings and the continuity of wholly positive actions [connected with it], are imagined to come about [in time] and be objectifiable,   [80–81]

In the same way as the potential for experience is not found, ever-fresh awareness also is not found. How is this? These forms of nonconceptual ever-fresh awareness belonging to the state of an Awakened One, purify all the concepts elaborated by the mind. Yet, due to grasping through thought and objectifying the flawless total field of events and meanings as well as the ongoing and immeasurable continuity of positive activities (connected with it, these forms of ever-fresh awareness) are thought of and imagined as coming into existence (as something). But,

> Since there is no causal basis for vajra-like (ever-fresh awareness), (our potential for experience, as causal basis, and ever-fresh awareness, as result) are alike regarding this similar condition (of nonexistence). And,   [82]

Also, if the foundation or motivating cause of conceptless ever-fresh awareness, which is called *vajra*, is the potential for experience of sentient beings, then since it was shown above that this potential itself does not exist and can't be found (when inquired into), then the cause here does not exist and the result also does not come about. Thus, since the two (potential for experience and ever-fresh awareness) are the same in not being found, ever-fresh awareness is not to be found just as the potential for experience is not to be found. Although the Mentalists say that a momentary, conceptless ever-fresh awareness ultimately does exist,[26] it is not to be found. Why?

> Since these supreme forms of vajra-like (ever-fresh aware-
> ness) that (thoroughly grasp) the total field of events and
> meanings, are without boundaries, they are not momen-
> tary events.   [83]

The nonconceptual ever-fresh awareness that fully grasps the
total field of events and meanings is excellent and supreme,
like a vajra. If characteristics such as these cannot be made
into an object for the mind, then how can one speak of
momentariness?

   B. Why is pure, though worldly, ever-fresh awareness not
to be found?[27]

> Since the source of pure, positive qualities is nonexistent
> like a reflection, ever-fresh awareness that deals with
> mundane matters does not exist.   [84]

Since the source of that which is positive, which completely purifies the three aspects (of actor, action, and object of
activity), is nonexistent like a reflection, how can pure,
though worldly, ever-fresh awareness that is based on this,
exist?

   6. Of the twelve major topics, the sixth is pointing out the
real meaning (grasped) after inquiring into (the above). It has
three aspects: (a) pointing out fundamental alikeness (at the
level) of thought; (b) fundamental alikeness (at the level) of
behavior; and (c) a summary of what defines the primordial
experience of pure and total presence.

   a. Fundamental alikeness (at the level) of thought has three
aspects: (i) fundamental alikeness because the two truths are
not divided and there is no acceptance and rejection; (ii) fundamental alikeness of truth and falsity, since there is no aversion to that which is objectionable and no longing for that
which is positive; and (iii) fundamental alikeness because
there is nothing for the mind to objectify, since one is free
from the four limiting conceptions.[28]

   a.i. Fundamental alikeness since there is no division into
two truths and nothing to accept or reject, is pointed out by
the following:

> Therefore, since what we define as "pure and total presence" and "lack of pure and total presence" are one in not existing, there is nothing to accept or reject.   [85]

It was demonstrated above that that which muddies the stream of awareness as well as its clarification are not to be found (if inquired into). Therefore, since what we define as Pure and Total Presence, i.e., the state of an Awakened One, and Lack of Pure and Total Presence i.e., the state of sentient beings, are one in not existing, there is no state of an Awakened One to be obtained and no status of sentient being to be rejected. If what is called the "ultimate" also does not exist, then how can there be terms that indicate "the ultimate is such and such"?

> In this sense, then, the terms for the ultimate, such as *non-existence of origination and cessation, fundamental alikeness, nonduality, beyond thought, openness, the total field of events and meanings, beyond conventional designations and language*, are all conventional designations. When the ultimate does not exist, then the state of a pervasive lack of clarity does not exist.   [86–88]

If what is called the "ultimate" does not exist, then how can there be terms that indicate that the "ultimate is such and such"? According to the sense (pointed out) above, all of these terms for the "ultimate," such as *nonexistence of origination and cessation, fundamental alikeness, nonduality, beyond thought, openness, the total field of events and meanings, free from conventional designations and language*, etc., are conventional explanations. In the real, definitive sense, the "ultimate" and "the state of a pervasive lack of clarity" do not exist.

> Saying that something ultimately is the case, is itself the state of a pervasive lack of clarity.   [89]

The "ultimate" or the "relative" are conventional designations belonging to the relative (i.e., conditioned) level of the state of a lack of clarity. In reality, in the realm of nonduality, how can there be a division into the two truths?

a.ii. Pointing out the fundamental alikeness of truth and falsity, since there is no aversion to the objectionable and no longing for the positive:

> One should not remain in a state wherein there is no doubt,
> nor eliminate a state of doubt.   [90]

Since the duality of true and false does not exist, then even when there is no doubt, having seen the truth, or when there is doubt, having not seen the truth, one should not try to stay with the truth or eliminate untruth. Why?

> Since there is no meditator and no total field of events and
> meanings (as object of meditation), there is neither doubt
> nor genuine insight.   [91]

Who fully grasps what, when ultimately there is no meditator who fully comprehends and no total field of events and meanings fully comprehended? Since there is no doubt, then in the absence of doubt there is no genuine insight. Also the canonical texts agree (that one should) "eliminate longing for what is positive."

a.iii. Pointing out fundamental alikeness since there is nothing for the mind to objectify and one is free from the four limiting conceptions:

> Since, if one inquires into our limiting conception, "en-
> tities," they are (found to be) nonexistent even as regards
> their apparitional nature,   [92]

As shown above, if one inquires into entities within our limiting conception, they are not to be found as having even an apparitional nature,

> Then even this nonexistence, which is dependent upon ex-
> istence, is nonexistent. Also, the nonexistence of this
> nonexistence does not exist.   [93]

If existence is not to be found, is there then nonexistence? If existence itself is not to be found, whose nonexistence is this nonexistence? Therefore, if existence is not to be found, one can't postulate a nonexistence based on this existence. Well, then, is it possible to speak of "nonexistence" in regard to this state of complete nonexistence in which nothing, by its very nature, comes into existence? It is not. Since what does not exist as any fact, which is not seen or heard, cannot be called or thought of as "nonexistent," even nonexistence does not exist as nonexistence.

> Since the limiting concepts do not exist, the middle (between these) does not exist. One does not remain even in a "middle." [94]

The nonexistence of the limiting conceptions of existence and nonexistence, etc., has been pointed out above. Then, if a limiting conception does not exist, what "middle" can there be? Even the middle does not exist. Since the middle does not exist, one cannot remain even in this middle.

b. Fundamental alikeness (at the level) of behaviour (is shown by the following):

> Just as the "Lotus-like Lord" of everything worldly does not reject anything, (all things) are seen as alike and present in utter sameness. [95]

"Powerful"[29] is spoken of in regard to actions for the sake of any excellent thing whatsoever that is desired in the world. (Further it means) that that which one possesses, one is able to use. "Rich" is spoken of in regard to the absence of avarice and the enjoyment of the excellent things desired. Although it seems that a lotus is stained by a red color, it is not stained or diminished (in its purity) by this new color. In the same way, although one is involved with the five excellent things desired in the world[30] and it seems that one is tainted by error, just as a lotus is not stained by coloring, one is not tainted by error. Therefore, one says, "Lotus-like Lord." Further, just as a lotus is not tainted by faults, (symbolized by) water, etc., since one is not tainted by error when one fully grasps the sense of what was pointed out above, one says, "Lotus-like Lord." If one is not tainted, like a lotus, this is also the meaning of, "not rejecting (anything) but engaging in the five pleasures." "Present in utter sameness" refers to faults and good qualities, since they are fundamentally alike, without any distinction. Since they are fundamentally alike and not distinguished (on this level), one remains in a state of not rejecting (anything).

> This very seeing as deceptive that which (is fundamentally not deceptive) is to be understood as deception.   [96]

If even sentient beings are not to be found, who is deceived? This very seeing (of things) as deceptive, which are not (themselves) deceptive, is to be understood as deception. Therefore,

> Even the teachings of the six (Hindu schools) and the deeds of the Lord of limitations are not rejected and regarded as negative.   [97]

Since even the teachings of the six Hindu teachers,[31] the factors that muddy the stream of awareness and that are an obstacle to a wholesome existence, the deeds of the Lord of limitations, etc., are not made an object for the mind, they are not thought of as bad and rejected.

> Since even engaging in skillful action and discernment do not exist, engaging in them is like the (activity) of the Lord of limitations.   [98]

In their not being found (if inquired into), there is no basis for what is defined as "engaging in skillful action and discernment." Since the activities of the Lord of limitations, as well as these, are the same in being unborn, engaging in them is on the same level.

> Having become proud through taking one's understanding as the best, superior to all, attachment and aversion arise, from which arguments come about. This is lack of awareness. The real point is not seen.   [99–100]

From the (standpoint of) being free from all philosophical views, attachment to the viewpoint even of "seeing reality as it is," is a fault. Ultimately, although both truth and falsity are not to be found, having become conceited in one's own view through pride, thinking, "I understand the truth through my own intelligence," there arises antipathy for the positions of others and attachment to one's own position. Then, although there is nothing called "truth" one says that my viewpoint is true; and although there is nothing known as "falsity," one says that the others' viewpoint is false and in error. This kind of arguing is ignorance. One doesn't see the real meaning of not conceiving of truth and falsity.

c. Summing up, pointing out what defines the primordial state of pure and total presence:

> As long as there is the agitated movement of the mind, there is the realm of the Lord of limitations. (This practice of pure and total presence) is a subtle path, in which one does not remain even in the states of the absence of movement of thought or of nonmovement. This middle path in which there is no deceptive appearance has been called the "primordial state of pure and total presence" by the Awakened Ones. [101–103]

One does not even remain in a state of the nonexistence of any conventional designations, such as either the "movement" or "nonmovement"[32] of thought and the identifiable characteristics with which it deals. The nonexistence of what appears as an object grasped by thought, such as "it is such," "something is felt," or "feeling has ceased," is the Middle Way. By directing the mind in such a manner towards the real meaning, since unparalleled pure and total presence is realized, it has been called the "primordial state of pure and total presence" by the Awakened Ones.

7. From the twelve topics, the seventh is putting the real meaning into practice, which also has two parts: (a) pointing out the obstacles to practice, and (b) pointing out the true meaning of practice.

a. Obstacles to practice (are shown as follows):

> Having eliminated holding on to form, identifiable characteristics, and wishfulness, while cultivating the three "gateways to freedom," is the activity of the Lord of limitations. Form (itself) is open-dimensional.
>
> [104–105]

Since nonconceptual cultivation is without any acceptance and rejection, if one eliminates the three obstacles of form, etc., and holds to the three "gateways to freedom," of openness, absence of identifiable characteristics, and desirelessness,[33] this is the activity of the Lord of limitations since one falls into the extremes of acceptance and rejection. Since form itself is open-dimensional, identifiable characteristics themselves without identifiable characteristics, and desire itself the absence of desire, there is nothing to eliminate.

> Eliminating the three paths of samsara while cultivating nirvana is also the activity of the Lord of limitations. This (kind of cultivation) is not the quiet nature of everything. There is not any (samsara) eliminated or actual state (of nirvana) sought.   [106–107]

That which sets up samsara is called "the path of samsara." Even the elimination of attachment, aversion, and ignorance, along with the cultivation and seeking of nirvana, are the very activity of the Lord of limitations. Thus, that type of cultivation does not understand the quiet nature of everything, since both the seeking of the path to nirvana and the eliminating of the way of samsara are not to be found and just do not exist.

> Nirvana, and so forth, the status (reached) and realm of vision of all the Noble Ones, do not exist apart from this very path.   [108]

Apart from the path taught here, which realizes the superior capacities—such as the realm of pure vision of the Noble Ones and the state that they have reached; nirvana (that is obtained) through not being conditioned by, as well as through abandoning, the obstacles spoken of (above); and so forth—there is no other path for realizing the status of an Awakened One.

   b. Pointing out the true meaning of cultivation has four aspects: (i) briefly pointing out the true sense of cultivation; (ii) a (brief) explanation of why, according to reason, (one ought) to so practice; (iii) pointing out the signs of proper

cultivation; and (iv) pointing out the logical reason for cultivating in this way.[34]

b.i. Pointing out the true sense of cultivation:

> When (a thought) arises one does not eliminate it, nor does
> one construct a support for the mind when no (thought)
> arises.   [109]

One does not eliminate thoughts when they arise, nor the
identifiable characteristics with which they deal; one does not
fashion a support for the mind on account of the nonarising
(of thought); nor does one realize an ultimate reality or goal.

b.ii. Why should one cultivate as above?

> (Even if) there stirs the slightest (thought) that is not (the
> dimension of knowledge called) Mañjuśrī, this itself is
> still that (dimension of knowledge). But one does not try
> to remain in that.   [110]

Why does one neither "eliminate" nor "remain"? The answer
is that Mañjuśrī refers to the ultimate content of what is,
which is (here metaphorically) called "gentle" because there is
no irritation; and since thoroughly comprehending it one becomes "lordly," one says "Gentle Lord" (Mañjuśrī).[35] One
may take even the slightest stirring of mistaken grasping after
identifiable characteristics as something other than the ultimate content of what is, i.e., Mañjuśrī. But, in that this itself is
also the ultimate content of what is, there is nothing to eliminate since it is not other than the very nature of the Noble
Mañjuśrī. What is this ultimate content like? It's not anything
at all; therefore, since there is no basis for remaining even in
the nature of Mañjuśrī, the ultimate content of what is, it says,
"one does not try to remain in that."

> Since one cannot obtain a foundation for meditation, one
> will not obtain any result by meditation.
> Grasping experience through thought, which is the sphere
> of operation of our "mind," is itself the ultimate content
> of what is.   [111–112]

Why is there no (goal) to bring into reality? Since both a mind
that meditates and an "ultimate content of what is" to be

meditated upon can't be found, one cannot obtain a basis or ground for meditation. Since that does not exist, who obtains a goal by what meditation? Therefore, there is no (goal) to bring into reality. The sphere of the operation of mind is itself the ultimate content of what is. Any perceptible quality of an object that appears, or construct of mind that is born, is not other than the ultimate content of what is. Thus it is shown to lack nothing. Any intended object[36] that appears in the sphere of operation of the mind is the ultimate content of what is. Therefore, any intended object that appears lacks nothing. If there is nothing wrong, why do sentient beings (wander in) samsara? Because they latch on to various identifiable characteristics. In order to point out that freedom from identifiable characteristics (means) not wandering in samsara, (there is the following):

> Since one is free from (seizing on) perceptible qualities,
> there does not exist anything that is better or worse. This
> supreme path is to be cultivated.   [113]

What is meant by a "perceptible quality"? Since the coming about of a perceptible quality, whether it be of a directly sensed object or a mental process regarding a past object, produces an awareness and a latching on to (that perceptible quality), there is the awareness of a perceptible quality that we term "perception."[37] Cultivating what truly is, is spoken of as "free from perceptible qualities" because there is no latching on to any such perceptible quality. Thus, to practice not latching on to such a perceptible quality is the supreme path, since one does not see things in terms of better or worse. Although the grasping of experience through thought arises, that there is no problem is (pointed out as follows):

> Since neither do conditioned events arise (on their own)
> nor do all configurations of events and meanings come
> about (dependently), all these are taken beyond the realm
> of frustration and suffering.
> When (one has thoroughly grasped that) there are no "en-
> tities," everything then (arises) as the total field of events

and meanings—understanding this is the supreme state of those who have overcome emotional conflicts.

[114–115]

All configurations of contingent events are, in their very fact of being, "unborn"; that is, since they do not even come about through external causes and conditions, they are characterized by being beyond the realm of suffering. Therefore, when one fully grasps or intrinsically knows this, there is no defect (to be found) in whatever thought or awareness arises. (This) intrinsic knowing or full grasp of the total field of events and meanings is called the "supreme state of having overcome emotional conflicts." It is (also) called the "supreme state of having overcome emotional conflicts," since it is the destruction of the enemy, the darkness of lack of awareness.[38]

> Space is unobjectifiable and is a mere name. That which is positive for an individual and that which is negative, being indivisible, do not arise. [116]

As an example of the meaning of what has been taught above (one says that such a method of cultivation) is like the sky. "The sky" is just a mere name; the reality indicated by the name cannot be objectified as having any defining characteristic. Therefore, that which is positive and negative, etc. cannot be divided into two, since they do not arise.

b.iv. An extensive explanation that one should practice thus, on account of it's having been logically established by the reasons shown above:

> The mind is not engaged in seeking nor is it directed towards anything. One is free from knowing and not knowing. [117]

One does not engage the mind in seeking something to affirm or reject, nor does one direct the mind towards any objective support. Since even mind itself is not to be found and one doesn't make a distinction between knowing and not knowing, it says, "free from knowing and not knowing."

There is neither picking out nor attending to (aids to meditation).[39] Delight in acceptance and rejection are alike in
not existing. Not objectifying (anything), and   [118]

Since both obstacles (to fully grasping) the true sense, as well
as the antidotes (for these), are indivisible, there is no attending to the antidotes. Neither does a person who delights in
acceptance and rejection exist. There is no setting up of obstacles and their antidotes, in that they are fundamentally alike,
equal. One does not objectify anything, and

> Remaining with the (understanding of) this alikeness, there
> is no creation of duality; one is beyond the realm of
> speech; there is neither activity nor inactivity; there is no
> accumulation (of merit) or diminution (of faults), etc.
>   [119]

Remaining with (the understanding) of fundamental alikeness, there is neither desire nor absence of desire; through not
making divisions there is also no fabrication of dualism. Since
there is no latching on to (thinking) "this is such and such,"
one does not verbalize anything; therefore one is free from
verbalization. There is no "having to do something," since
there is no striving. There is also no inactivity, since one does
not find any problem with actions through the three gates (of
body, "speech," and mind). There is (also) no bringing to
fulfillment the two accumulations,[40] just as in the saying, "In
the ultimate content of what is, there is nothing to increase or
diminish."

b.iii. How do the signs of proper cultivation arise?

> One's mind is not engaged in seeking anything. One is not
> disturbed by anything, knowing the fundamental alike-
> ness (of everything); and   [120]

Practicing unerringly as taught above, when there arises the
knowledge of fundamental alikeness, the signs (of proper
practice) arise.

> There is no fear of intoxication by objects or attachment to
> anything. One does not avoid nor dwell on (anything).
>   [121]

There is neither dullness nor intoxication due to one's normal awareness of objects, nor desire and attachment to anything. Since they are without essence, there is no fear of, or desire for, anything. Therefore, one does not avoid anything. Since there is no delighting in and then being attached to anything, one does not dwell on anything.

> The ways of overcoming (limitations), the facets (of pure and total presence), the four forms of ever-fresh awareness of the alikeness (of everything), which are undisturbed (by negative conditions), are known in this (practice).   [122]

The four forms of ever-fresh awareness that thoroughly grasp the fundamental alikeness (that characterizes) the ultimate content of what is and that are not conditioned by any obstacles; the thirty-seven facets of pure and total presence; the ten ways of overcoming (limitations), etc.;[41] and that which is positive for an individual (relatively speaking), as well as all the positive qualities that belong to the level of the ultimate goal,[42] are known quickly through the reflexive flash of knowing that gives awareness its quality, and brought together in the teaching of the true sense of cultivation.

> Cultivating the all-encompassing field of experience (is) this path; if one has cultivated otherwise, the transparent clarity (of the field) will not come about.   [123]

Since all entities are included within the expanse of our potential for experience, cultivating this potential itself according to the sense taught above develops into an unerring path. If one practices otherwise, despite this practice the knowledge and clarity intrinsic (to thoroughly grasping) the true sense will not come about.

8. Of the twelve topics, the eighth is: what are the special methods taught for fully grasping the real meaning? The answer is:

> To really get (the meaning) through symbolic means is also "pure and total presence": so has the Teacher proclaimed.   [124]

For example, just as one gestures to give the meaning, "come over here" by a symbolic gesture with the right hand; so, by the activity of focusing the mind one can fully comprehend, just as it is, what is meant by "nonaction."[43] Moreover, since this makes for the realization of pure and total presence, the Teacher, the Awakened One, has proclaimed, "It is pure and total presence."

> (The symbolic means) are here the foundation for the activation and cultivation of pure and total presence itself.
>
> [125]

The "symbolic encounters" and "contemplations" (pointed out) next are the basis, or motivating cause, for the activation and cultivation of the absolutely genuine, primordial state of pure and total presence.

> Having made use of the three "symbolic encounters" that are indicative of (facets of the existence of an Awakened One), and made firm the three contemplations,   [126]

When one has not arrived at the real sense of "nonaction," (one employs) the contemplation by focusing without thought; the contemplation that is present everywhere like the sky; and the contemplation of A, OM, etc., the "causal" contemplation, which are the "three contemplations."[44] In being the defining characteristic of the three contemplations, "firm" refers to not coming under (the power of) disturbing conditions. "Indicative" means, for example, that since that which indicates (the presence of) a king is his symbol, all the actions of a king are done using this symbol. Similarly, through the symbols indicative of an Awakened One, all the charismatic activities are performed. The symbolic encounter indicative of "primordial contact" is called the "supreme symbolic encounter"; the symbolic encounter indicative of "primordial experiencing" is called the "symbolic encounter based on commitments"; and the symbolic encounter indicative of "primordial action" is called the "symbolic encounter through activity."⁴⁵ Having had, as well as developed, these three symbolic encounters, then, through the symbolic encounter indicative of "primordial communication,"

> Primordial experience itself is activated in the "symbolic encounter with the ultimate content of what is."⁴⁶ One should visualize and recite the heart mantra (of the divinity that represents that). [127]

"Contemplations" and "symbolic encounters" are themselves the ultimate content of what is. Without separating oneself from these, also by activating the intent (to experience pure and total presence) along with concentrating on and reciting the heart-mantra of a divinity, the ultimate primordial state of pure and total presence will arise. How will it come about? By practicing as above for a long time. When one has made such a practice palpably real, then there will arise the reflexive flash of knowing that gives awareness its quality, the thorough grasp of reality that "sees that there does not exist anything apart from one's own potential for experience itself appearing."⁴⁷ One will also come to this thorough knowledge through the arising of the accumulation of merit that purifies one's obstacles, along with the above cultivation.

9. Pointing out that without fully taking hold of the primordial state of pure and total presence, freedom will not be obtained and positive qualities will come to an end:

> By this "cultivation of the commitment to what is indestructible" all paths are unerringly cultivated. [128]

As pointed out above, since the potential for experience is, in actuality, the ultimate content of what is, (one speaks of) "vajra." The being who is unerringly intent on this is called "Vajrasattva." Experiencing, itself, when envisaging things wrongly appears as the all-pervasive muddying of the stream of awareness; while when envisaging things as they are, it appears as the various ways of being free. Therefore, it is shown that "all paths are unerringly cultivated."

> If anything positive for the individual, whatever it may be,
>   has not been taken up by the way of acting (symbolized
>   by) Samantabhadrī,   [129]

If one understands and thoroughly grasps all that one does
according to what has been pointed out above, since it is then
all wholly positive, one speaks of "Samantabhadrī." Since this
is the place of origin of all superior capacities without exception, then just as a child comes from a mother, one speaks of
this in the feminine. The above reality, empowered as a female
divinity, is referred to as "Samantabhadrī." She is considered
to be real discernment itself.[48] If any (positive activity) has
not been taken up by discernment,

> Then the way of acting (symbolized by) Samantabhadra be-
>   comes the activity of the Lord of limitations—in which
>   case it will reach its limit and be exhausted.   [130]

Since the skillful method of acting in the supreme, comprehensive approach is positive for oneself and others, one
speaks of "Samantabhadra." Also, since all one's ways of
acting through the three "gates," which have been taken up
by the above discernment, are positive, one (also) speaks of
"Samantabhadrī." Thus, if all one's ways of acting have not
been taken up by the above discernment, they will not become wholly positive. Then, since even all skillful activity
done for the benefit of oneself and others is found to be the
mere result of worldly desire, it will reach its limit and finally
be nonexistent:

> On the path that possesses this (primordial state of pure
>   and total presence), even the activity of the Lord of
>   limitations is said to be the activity of this pure and total
>   presence.   [131]

Actions through the three "gates," as well as all configurations of events and meanings, inner and outer, are limited and
uncertain, since from the mere understanding or lack of
understanding (of them) comes the motivating cause of that
which muddies the stream of awareness or its clarification.

10. Pointing out that even the arousal of more intense interest (in this primordial state) leads to many superior abilities:

> Intense interest in the meaning of this, moreover, has been
> praised by the Victorious One as "great, pure and total
> presence."   [132]

Because intense interest and conviction in the true sense of what has been pointed out above is "great, pure and total presence," this very dedication to, and knowledge of, just this has been praised by the Awakened One: "This is great, pure and total presence."

> By the mere activation of this source, the Awakened One
> has proclaimed, one will overcome the (limitations repre-
> sented by) the host of the Lord of limitations, as well as
> the Śrāvakas, who are the object of veneration of the tri-
> ple world and its rulers.   [133]

By the mere activation of this primordial state that is the birthplace of all superior abilities, it is said that one will over-come (the limitations represented by) the host of the Lord of limitations, as well as the Śrāvakas, who are an object of rev-erence in the world. That is, the objects of reverence of the beings of the triple world together with their lords, Brahma and Indra, are the Śrāvakas.[49]

> The greatest skillful action is this hidden activity of these
> committed to pure and total presence.   [135]

Although the great skillful action that makes unparalleled pure and total presence real, is understood and put into action by those who are committed to this primordial state, it is not known by the Śrāvakas, etc. Therefore, it is just this which is naturally hidden (from the Śrāvakas, etc.).

> If this (state of pure and total presence) did not exist, then
> the Victorious One could not make his appearance,[50] and
> it would then be impossible that the three approaches to
> the teaching be taught.   [136]

If this state of pure and total presence pointed out above were not thoroughly grasped or didn't exist, the state of an Awakened One could not be realized. If there were no Awakened One, it would be impossible for the three approaches to the teaching to be taught by another.

> In a mere instant, by the power of trusting confidence,
> moreover, one quickly becomes the youthful Mañjuśrī.
>
> [137]

Mañjuśrī actually also is this, since by thoroughly grasping this, (his status) is realized.

> Also, while the supreme commitments of the supreme, comprehensive approach to the teachings are kept and the hidden dimensions of existence[51] entered, all commitments and ethical behavior are protected and (those committed to pure and total presence) greatly praised as a noble object for offerings.   [138–9]

As pointed out above, this is so because there is no superior ability which is not included in this primordial state of pure and total presence. Therefore, from this primordial state one obtains countless accumulations of merit. How is this? Because

> If the merit of the state of pure and total presence had form,
> even the extent of space would be too small a container
> for it, the Victorious Ones have equally proclaimed.
>
> [140–1]

11. Pointing out that those who have gone wrong are the object of compassion:

> Individual beings have been born, are being born, and will
> be born in various forms of life, and thus have come
> under the power of the stream of birth.   [142]

Since they are born each through the power of karma, one speaks of "individual beings." The various births in the six forms of life are connected one after the other: (sentient beings) have been born previously, are being born now, and will be born later. Since the continuity of births is uninterrupted, they have come under the power of birth.

> Through not understanding what the grasping of experience through thought ultimately is, one is deceived by this grasping. The stream of thought continues, and so there is no (opportunity) to turn away from deluded thought later on. [143]

Through not knowing what the grasping of experience through thought, which is one's "mind," ultimately is, by this mistaken grasping one deceives oneself. Since the stream of this mistaken grasping continues uninterruptedly, there will be no opportunity to understand what is genuinely real and turn away from this mistaken grasping. For example, since (this) is like a dream in which one is deceived by the dream (into thinking it is real), or like a magic show in which one is deceived by an illusion, it is said,

> The illusory beings who are deceived by illusions such as an illusory elephant, by those who are skilled in the art of illusion, also lose their dreamlike happiness, just as when one is deceived by a dream (into thinking it is real). Since those who have come under the power of dreams [144-5]
> Reject this path and look to other paths that are extreme, and teach (that) as what they call the "unerring path," they are fit for a compassionate (response). They are like those who say stone is gold.[52] The compassion of the compassionate ones (is spontaneous), their minds being conditioned by commiseration.
>
> [146-7]

Rejecting the path pointed out above and not able to (follow) the supreme, comprehensive approach as it is, (those who are deceived) have the flaw of falling into extreme and limited conceptions, (which lead to) various philosophical positions. Therefore, they see as the path what is other than the supreme, comprehensive approach and teach, "(this) is the unerring path." This is like those who say stone is gold. (The verse) has the meaning that they are fit for compassion, and

that commiseration arises spontaneously in the compassionate Noble Ones, because of their compassion. For example,
the mind is agitated by a pleasing object and becoming caught
up in (the thought of that object), one becomes powerless (to
abandon it); thus one speaks of "thought or mind being conditioned by an object." Similarly the "mind" of the compassionate one is conditioned by compassion and one says,
"conditioned by compassion in that commiseration spontaneously arises."

> These sentient beings who suffer because of the temporal
>   circumstances and do not exercise (discernment) during
>   these last 500 years of the teaching,[53]
> Have difficulty understanding the pure teaching, and going
>   by mere words, do not (understand it) properly.
>   [148–9]

Since they do not exercise their power of discernment, sentient beings suffer because of their temporal circumstances,
(since they live) in the last 500 years of the teaching. (These
beings) who think about the teaching, having difficulty in
thoroughly grasping what the faultless, unerring teaching of
the One Who Has Come Through refers to, go by and fix on
the words of the teaching, but not their actual sense. What is
referred to is like gold (hidden) in a dungeon; words are like a
lamp. Although one seeks the gold that is being referred to by
the lamp of the words, just as that lamp is not the gold, one
should know that the words are not what they refer to. But,
one takes the word as what it actually refers to, and

> The various points of view (that result) are confirmed ac-
>   cording to each one's own capacity, etc. One is stirred up
>   by this river of misunderstanding and separated from the
>   yogic ambrosia that is the vital essence of the teaching.
>   [150–1]

Those who proceed according to a confirmation based on the
capacity of their deluded understanding, holding various per-
verse points of view, are thus agitated and carried away by the
river of this lack of understanding. Therefore, they are sepa-

rated from engaging in and developing the unerring yoga that is like ambrosia, what was really meant by the One Who Has Come Through.

12. Dedication for (the sake of creating) a foundation of positive qualities:

> Therefore, although this noble hidden dimension of primordial experiencing, the excellent path taught by the Victorious Ones,
> Is the extra-ordinary sphere of operation of the primordial experience of all the Victorious Ones, [152-3]

Since Mañjuśrīmitra's understanding is not the same as the total understanding of an Awakened One, the latter is extra-ordinary. Yet,

> I have validated it (for myself) by virtue of (long) experience and noncontradictory valid means of knowledge. [154]

The teacher, having accustomed himself for a long time to the real meaning, the hidden primordial experience of the Awakened Ones, has (here) set it forth according to the three valid means of knowledge: oral instruction, authoritative texts, and the power of meditation.[54]

> By composing this (work) on the excellent path of nonduality for the sake of sentient beings,
> May, in a single moment, in all the places of birth of sentient beings,
> Obstacles decrease and this primordial experience of all the Victorious Ones spread. [155-7]

By composing (this work) that briefly points out, for the sake of sentient beings, this excellent path of nonduality, (which is like) a trace left by the Awakened Ones of the three times, may (this) pure intention not be diminished by obstacles in all the temporal and spatial situations of all sentient beings. May this core of meaning, which has been taken to heart by all the Awakened Ones, increase and be thoroughly grasped by all sentient beings. This is the dedication.

Thus is completed *The Discussion under Twelve Headings* of the forty verses of *Cultivating the Primordial State of Pure and Total Presence*, written by Mañjuśrīmitra, the teacher from Sri Lanka, following the authoritative texts (of the Sems sde).

APPENDIX 1

BYANG CHUB KYI SEMS BSGOM PA

'phags pa 'jam dpal gzhon nur gyur pa la phyag 'tshal lo

bdag med gnyis nyid bde gshegs mi rtog ye shes chos dbyings sku
   brnyes pa   [1]

kun gyi rang bzhin zhi ba 'di la gsal zhing bla med lam mchog ste
                                                         [2]

mi ldog sa la sogs te[1] dbang bcu rgyal ba kun dang gcig brnyes pa
                                                          [3]

gnas gsum mnyam nyid de la mtshan med yid kyis rab tu dad pas[2]
   mos   [4]

ston pa 'jig rten sgron mar gyur pa kun gyis mtshungs par rab
   bsngags pa   [5]

chos la chos kyi snying por gyur pa 'jam dpal gzhon nu'i[3] snying po
   nyid   [6]

bde gshegs ma lus yum du gyur pas rgyal ba kun gyi lam gcig go [7]

tshul khrims la sogs pha rol phyin lam spyod pa rgya mtsho'i gzhir
   gyur pa   [8]

rnam dag byang chub sems kyi ngang tshul bsgoms dang yon tan
   khyad par ni   [9]

blo ldan nam zhig sems kyi dam pa de ni mngon du gyur pa na [10]

de la sku gsum mchog tu gyur pas[4] chos kyi sku zhes rgyal bas
   gsungs   [11]

shes byed dam par gyur pas[5] shes rab spyan zhes kyang ni de la bya
                                                             [12]

rdo rtse mo mchog nyid mi rtog ye shes de yang de nyid do   [13]

ji snyed 'phags pa'i rnam grol chos su bsnyad pa de dag thams cad
   kyang   [14]

byang chub sems nyid rdzogs las[6] de yi yon tan de dag de las byung
                                                            [15]

'phags pa'i rigs chen 'chi med byang chub sems dpa' de dag thams
   cad kyang   [16]

de med mi 'byung de phyir de ni rnam grol mchog gi lam nyid
do   [17]
des na[7] kun tu rdo rje sems dpa' ci 'drar bsgom par bya bar
'gyur   [18]
phra zhing shes dka' drang srong chen po'i lam 'di mi-rtog rtog las
'das   [19]
brtag par dka' zhing bstan par dka' la brjod pa'i tha snyad rnams
dang bral   [20]
tshig gis mi phebs gzhan dang byis pa kun gyi spyod yul[8] ma yin
yang   [21]
ston pa nges pa'i lung dang bla ma rnams kyi man ngag[9] don 'dir
blta   [22]
mngon sum la sogs rgyu yis[10] dngos po 'jig cing grub pa'i mtha'
dpyod[11] pa   [23]
de nyid rtog pa'i rgyun 'brangs spyod[12] yul tshad mar bzhag nas
blos[13] 'jig byed[14]   [24]
rtog mtha' med phyir dpyod mtha' med de snying po med na tshad
mar gang   [25]
de phyir 'jig rten brtags pa'i tha snyad rnal 'byor lam 'dir mi dgos so
                                                                                [26]
dngos po mtha' yi rgyu ni lo rgyus dag las lam 'dir brtags par bya
                                                                                [27]
skye bo kun gyi sems la mngon snang phyi nang grags pa'i chos 'di
ni   [28]
'dzin pa drug gi ji ltar mthong zhing brtag pa de ltar ma yin khrul
                                                                                [29]
rang gi rtog pas myos[15] shing gzung ba de bzhin bden par gyur na
ni[16]   [30]
de dag dngos po med rtog[17] dgra bcom 'dra bar grol[18] 'gyur pa yi[19]
rigs   [31]
de dag dus dgras 'joms dang sdug bsngal nyen las des 'khrul mngon
par 'gyur   [32]
gzhan du skye mched sgo nas rig pa de dag tshad mar gyur na
ni   [33]
de dag[20] tshad mar gyur pas 'phags pa'i lam de su la dgos mi
'gyur   [34]
lam de rnam grol[21] lam du bstan cing dbang po'i shes pas mi thar ti
                                                                                [35]
sdug bsngal 'ga' yang mi 'jil rnam rig shes te nyon mongs 'byung
ba'i gnas   [36]

de phyir skye bas mthong ba de dag 'khrul par[22] mngon zhes rgyal
bas gsungs   [37]
des na[23] 'di dag 'khrul pa'i dbang gis ji ltar snang bar 'gyur zhe na[24]
                                                                [38]
kun tu rtog can yang dag ma yin kun tu rtog pas rtsol med
nyams   [39]
blo gros phyin ci log tu gyur cing ma rig rkyen gyi[25] dbang song bas
                                                                [40]
sems dang sems las byung ba de nyid lus gsum don du snang ba
yin   [41]
'du byed sna tshogs dag gis[26] bag chags bsags las gang goms mthu
brtas tshe   [42]
sems nyid yul dang lus 'drar snang ba rus pas gang ba bzhin du
snang   [43]
bag chags bsags pa'i rgyun las[27] dmigs skyes yid la[28] brtags pa'i bdag
ni med[29]   [44]
'du byed mthu yis bsgribs shing phra ba ma mthong de las rnam rig
skye   [45]
rgyun dang bcas pa'i sems kyi mthu ni ma rtogs rtog pa'i rjes
'brangs nas   [46]
de las[30] zag bcas rang bzhin rtog pas bdag dang chos rnams rgyas
par byed   [47]
ldan[31] par 'byung ba shin tu phra bar rgyu ba de ni ma mthong las[32]
                                                                [48]
bdag tu lta sogs mu stegs lta ba sna tshogs skye zhing thar pa
rtog   [49]
sems 'di las rnams mtha' yas gnas gyur bag chags mtha' med nges pa
med   [50]
bag chags brtas shing sad par byed pa'i rkyen yang rnam pa sna
tshogs te   [51]
rkyen 'gas bag chags 'ga' zhig smin nas mi yi rgyud kyi lus snang
la[33]   [52]
rkyen gzhan dag gis bag chags gzhan sad byas tshe 'gyur ba'i mthu
mthong nas   [53]
dbang phyug la sogs byed par 'dod de[34] lam des mi zhi grol mi 'gyur
                                                                [54]
rnal byor lam bslad the tshom rgyu yang[35] rgyun 'di phra ba ma
rtogs skyes   [55]
bdag tu brtags pas yongs su[36] bsgribs te 'phags pa'i rigs dang rnam
par bral   [56]

chos su btags pas sdug bsngal sna tshogs 'byung zhing ngan song
    srid par 'gyur   [57]
rnam shes de yang 'du byed rgyun las³⁷ mtshan ma tha dad 'dzin pas
    na   [58]
las kyi khyad par dag gis brgyad du snang gi³⁸ rigs la tha dad
    med   [59]
de phyir sems kyi skad cig dang po de la lus and chos kun gnas
                                                              [60]
de la bsam pa zhen phyir phyi ma de la de 'byung de la snang³⁹
                                                              [61]
rang sems rgyun las 'phags pa skye bo chos ni gzhan na yod ma yin
                                                              [62]
rgyud drug rigs las⁴⁰ de yang sna tshogs de dang rang gi ting 'dzin
    no   [63]
sems rgyun de la⁴¹ phyogs kyang cung zad med pas gcig la brten
    med de   [64]
de la phyogs med phyir na mtha' yas zhing rnams thams cad⁴² bdag
    gi lus   [65]
bdag gi lus ni mtha' yas zhing dang skye bo'i lus su rab snang yang
                                                              [66]
sems dang bag chags gcig min tha dad ma yin brtag par rab tu dka'
                                                              [67]
'di kun rten cing 'brel 'byung tshul te skye dang 'gag par 'gyur zhes
    pa   [68]
tshig pa'i sa bon bzhin du med las med pa mi 'byung rgyu 'bras med
                                                              [69]
dngos por zhen cing rgyu dang 'bras bu so sor⁴³ rtog⁴⁴ pa'i sems
    nyid ni   [70]
rgyu dang rkyen du snang ste de gnyis med phyir skye dang 'jig pa
    med   [71]
skye 'jig med phyir bdag gzhan med de 'chi 'pho med phyir rtag
    chad med   [72]
des na 'khrul 'khor med cing mya ngan 'das pa med pa nyid du
    mngon   [73]
gnas kyi skad cig nam yang mi 'bral de tshe mnyam 'gyur de med
    med   [74]
yang dag ma yin rtog pas bskyed phyir bag chags yod pa ma yin
    dang   [75]
spyod yul med phyir kun gzhi med cing rnam rig de yang med pa
    yin⁴⁵   [76]

phyogs rnams med phyir[46] dmigs dang gnas med rnam par[47] rig pa ji
ltar skye   [77]
de phyir sems 'di yod med mtha' las 'das shing gcig dang du mar
bral   [78]
bde gshegs byang chub med phyir de yi rdzu 'phrul sgyu 'drar
'khrul la snang   [79]
de bzhin dag pa'i ye shes de dag shin tu dge ba'i rgyun[48] nyid dang
     [80]
chos kyi dbyings nyid la ni de dag dmigs shing skye bar brtags pa
yang   [81]
rdo rje'i gnas med phyir na mnyam gnas rang bzhin 'drar gyur dang
     [82]
chos dbyings rdo rje rtse mo de dag phyogs nyid med pas skad cig
min   [83]
dag pa'i dge rtsa gzugs brnyan med pas[49] 'jig rten ye shes yod mi
'gyur   [84]
de phyir byang chub ma chub mtshan nyid med par gcig pas blang
dor med   [85]
don de'i tshul gyis don dam rnam grangs skye 'gag med dang
mnyam nyid dang   [86]
gnyis med bsam 'das stong nyid[50] chos dbyings brjod dang tha
snyad bral la sogs   [87]
bstan pa de kun tha snyad yin te don dam med cing kun sgrib[51] med
     [88]
dam tshul gyis lam nyid 'di[52] 'dra zhes pa de nyid kun sgrib[53]
yin   [89]
the tshom yod med chos ni gang la'ang spong zhing gnas par mi
byed do   [90]
sgom dang[54] chos dbyings med phyir som nyi med la dam par blta
ba'ang[55] med   [91]
de ltar dngos po'i[56] mtha' rnams brtags[57] pas[58] rang bzhin sgyu
ma'ang med 'gyur phyir   [92]
yod la ltos pa'i med pa[59] med de bzhin de[60] med pa'i med[61] pa'ang
med   [93]
mtha rnams med phyir dbus med dbus la'ang gnas par mi byed do[62]
     [94]
gang la 'jig rten dbang phyug padma kun kyang mi spong 'drar[63]
mnyam gnas   [95]
chos la 'khrul par mthong ba de nyid[64] 'khrul pa yin par rab rtogs te
     [96]

drug gis bstan pa[65] bdud kyi las kyang mi 'dor ngan du mi rtogs[66] go
                                                                    [97]
shes rab thabs kyi spyod pa'ang[67] mi gnas phyir na bdud kyi[68] 'dra
    bar spyod   [98]
rang gi shes pa dam par byas shing[69] kun las rgyal te de bsnyems nas
                                                                    [99]
'dod chags zhe sdang skyes nas rtsod 'byung gti mug yin te don mi
    mthong   [100]
ji srid yid kyi[70] g.yo ba de srid bdud kyi yul te phra ba'i lam   [101]
g.yo dang mi g.yo tha snyad mi gnas gnas pa la yang gnas par mi
    byed do   [102]
snang med dbu ma'i lam de byang chub sems zhes bde gshegs pas[71]
    gsungs   [103]
gzugs dang mtshan ma smon par 'dzin pa rab tu spangs nas ni   [104]
rnam thar sgo[72] gsum po bsgom pa'ang bdud kyi las te gzugs nyid
    stong pa'o   [105]
'khor ba'i lam gsum spang[73] zhing mya ngan 'das lam bsgom pa'ang
    bdud nyid de   [106]
de nyid chos kun[74] rang bzhin ma zhi rang bzhin brtsal spangs gar
    gar mi gans   [107]
'phags pa kun gyi yul dang gnas kyang 'das sogs lam nyid[75] gzhan
    na med   [108]
ldang dang mi ldang ched du mi spong sems rten mi 'cha' mngon du
    min   [109]
'jam dpal ma yin rdul tsam g.yo ba de nyid[76] de yin der mi gnas
                                                                   [110]
bsgom pa'i sa mi rnyed phyir bsgoms pas 'bras bu[77] rnyed par[78] mi
    'gyur te   [111]
sems kyi spyod yul shes pa de dag chos rnams kyi ni chos nyid yin
                                                                   [112]
rnam bral gang la'ang[79] mchog dang tha ma med par lam chog 'di
    sgom[80] mo   [113]
'du byed ma skyes chos kun 'byung[81] med chos rnams shin tu[82] mya
    ngan 'das   [114]
dngos med de tshe kun kyang chos kyi dbyings shes[83] dgra dcom
    rab 'byor yin   [115]
nam mkha' mi dmigs ming[84] tsam dge dang mi dger 'byed med skye
    ba'ang med   [116]
rtsol bar yid la mi byed gang la'ang sems med shes dang mi shes bral
                                                                   [117]

dran dang 'byed med spang len[85] gang la'ang 'ga' dang mtshungs[86]
mi dmigs shing [118]
mnyams gnas[87] gnyis su brtag[88] med brjod bral bya dang mi bya[89]
sogs bri[90] med [119]
ched du rtsol bral[91] yid la mi byed cis kyang mi 'khrugs mnyam shes
dang [120]
gang la'ang chags dang yul gyis[92] myos sgrag med de mi 'bral mi
gnas shing [121]
mi 'phrogs mnyam shes bzhi po phyogs dang pha rol phyin rnams
dir shes te [122]
sems kyi dbyings su sgom[93] pas lam 'di gzhan du[94] 'od gsal mi 'gyur
ro [123]
(sems kyi dbyings su bsgoms pas lam gyi phug na 'dug pa de yin
[123]
gzhan du bsgom pas 'od gsal don nyid gsal zhing rig par mi 'gyur
ro[95] [123a])
brda can yang dag len pa'ang byang chub[96] yin zhes ston pas rab
gsungs phyir [124]
de la 'di ni byang chub sems nyid bskyed cing bsgom pa'i gnas yin te
[125]
ting 'dzin gsum po brtan[97] par byas nas rtags kyi phyag rgya gsum
bcings nas [126]
chos kyi phyag rgya chen por sems nyid bskyed[98] de snying po
brjod cing bsgom[99] [127]
rdo rje sems dpa' bsgoms pas rnam grol[100] lam kun ma nor bsgoms
pa[101] yin [128]
kun tu bzang mo'i spyod pas ma zin dge ba'i chos ni gang yang rung
[129]
kun tu bzang po'i spyod pa'ang[102] bdud kyi las te zad cing mthar
thug 'gyur [130]
de dang ldan pa'i las ni bdud kyi las kyang byang chub spyod par
gsungs [131]
don 'dir mos pa de yang byang chub che[103] zhes rgyal bas rab tu
bsngags [132]
gnas 'dir bskyed pa tsam gyis 'jig rten gsum po bla mar bcas[104] pa
yi[105] [133]
mchod nas nyan thos bdud kyi sde rnams zil gyis gnon zhes sangs
rgyas[106] gsungs [134]
thabs chen byang chub sems dpa'[107] rnams kyi[108]gsang ba'i spyod
pa'ang[109] 'di nyid do [135]

'di med¹¹⁰ rgyal ba rnam par snang mdzad theg pa gsum ston mi srid
do   [136]
skad cig¹¹¹ dad pa'i¹¹² shugs bskyed de yang myur du 'jam dpal
gzhon nur gyur   [137]
dkyil 'khor gsang bar zhugs shing theg chen dam tshig mchog kyang
bsrung ba¹¹³ yin   [138]
tshul khrims sdom pa kun kyang bsrungs¹¹⁴ shing sbyin gnas dam
par rab tu bsngags   [139]
de phyir byang chub sems kyi bsod nams de la gal te¹¹⁵ gzugs yod
na   [140]
nam mkha' bar snang 'di¹¹⁶ yang snod du chung¹¹⁷ zhes rgyal bas
mtshungs par¹¹⁸ gsungs   [141]
skye bo skye ba sna tshogs dag¹¹⁹ skyes shing skye dang¹²⁰ skye
'gyur skye ba'i rgyun gyi dbang song bas¹²¹   [142]
rtog¹²² mtha' mi shes rtog pas bslus shing rtog¹²³ pa'i rgyun 'brangs
'khrul pa'i rtog las phyir zlog¹²⁴ med gyur¹²⁵   [143]
sgyu ma'i sgyu shes dag cing¹²⁶ sgyu ma'i glang po 'dra bar sgyu
mas rmongs pa'i sgyu ma rnams   [144]
rmi lam gyis bslad bzhin du rmi yi¹²⁷ bde ba'ang¹²⁸ nyams shing rmi
lam dbang du song ba'i rmi lam pa¹²⁹   [145]
lam 'di spangs¹³⁰ zhing mtha' dang lam gzhan lam du bltas nas ma
nor lam zhes ston pa de   [146]
de dag rdo la gser bzhin thugs rjer rung zhing thugs rje'i¹³¹ thugs
rjes kye ma 'bros¹³² pa yin   [147]
shin tu ma sbyangs dus kyi mnar ba'i skye bo lnga brgya tha ma la
                                                                      [148]
gsung rab dri med rtogs dka' dag la sgra bzhin spyod dang tshul
bzhin min   [149]
rang gi blo gros stobs bzhin 'jug pa la sogs lta ba sna tshogs dag
                                                                      [150]
mi shes chu bos g.yengs shing gsung gi nying khu¹³³ bdud rtsi'i¹³⁴
rnal 'byor bral   [151]
de phyir rgyal bas gsungs pa'i lam mchog¹³⁵ thugs kyi gsang ba dam
pa¹³⁶ 'di   [152]
kun tu rgyal ba rnams kyi thugs kyi¹³⁷ spyod yul¹³⁸ thun mong ma
yin yang   [153]
goms pa'i mthu yis mi 'gal tshul du tshad ma dag las rab bsgrubs te
                                                                      [154]
'gro ba'i don du mi gnyis lam mchog 'di ni rab bgyis thams cad
du¹³⁹   [155]

skye bo'i[140] skye gnas thams cad du yang skad cig tu[141]   [156]
mi mthun phyogs kyis mi nyams rgyal ba kun gyi thugs 'di[142] rab
    rgyans shog   [157]
'jam dpal bshes gnyen gyis mdzad pa rdzogs so
rgya gar gyi mkhan po shri sim ha dang bod kyi lo tsa ba bai ro tsa
na rak shi tas bsyur[143]

NOTES FOR APPENDIX 1

Abbreviations

V.	= *Vairocana rgyud 'bum*
D.	= *sDe sge bstan 'gyur*
P.	= *Peking bstan 'gyur*
M.	= Mi-pham's commentary
DN.	= *gDams ngag mdzod*
comm.	= commentary

For bibliographic references, see Introduction, Section I.

1. V. pa
2. V. dad pas rab tu
3. D. nu
4. V. pa, D. par
5. D. pa
6. D pas
7. D. de nas
8. V. add thun mong
9. D.P. read bla ma dam pa rnams dyi gdams ngag de nyid; V. reads bla
    ma rnams kyi nyams
10. D.P. yi
11. D.P. dpyad
12. D.P. dpyod
13. D.P.V. etc. read blo yis
14. D.P.V. etc. add de
15. M. myongs
16. D.P.V. read bden gyur na

17. D.P. rtogs
18. P. omits
19. V. reads 'gyur bar
20. D.P.V. de nyid
21. V. rnal 'byor
22. V. pa yin par
23. D. de na, P. des ni, V. des; D.P. add de las
24. DN. omit zhe na
25. V. gyis
26. D. comm. gi
27. D. P. la
28. M. las
29. D.P. read bdag med pa
30. DN. V. la
31. DN. bden
32. DN. bas
33. D.P. ba
34. DN. pas; D.P. add nyes pa
35. D.P. omit rgyu yang
36. D.P.V. omit yongs su
37. D.P.V. la
38. DN. gis
39. D. (but not D. comm.) reads de la bsam pa zhen pa'i phyir na phyi ma phyi ma de la snang
40. V. la
41. D.P. las; DN. ni
42. D.P.V. omit thams cad
43. D.P.V. read 'bras bur, omit so sor
44. V. zhen
45. D.P. bzhin
46. D.P. cing
47. DN. V. shes
48. DN. rgyu; V. dag pa'i rgyu
49. V. phyir
50. D.P. omit stong nyid
51. V. bsgribs
52. D.P. omit nyid 'di
53. V. bsgribs
54. D.P. read sgom pa dang ni
55. D.P. la yang; V. omits la yang

56. D.P.V. po
57. D. rtags, P. btags
58. D.P.V. dang
59. D.P. add 'ang, V. yang
60. D.P.V. omit bzhin de
61. D.P. omit pa'i med; B. reads: yod la ltos pa'i med pa rang med de med pa'i bden pa'ang med
62. D.P. la
63. DN. 'dra
64. V. dag
65. DN. pa'i
66. D.P. rtog
67. D.P.V. la
68. DN. rtsi
69. D.P. pa, DN. te
70. V. omit yid kyi
71. D.P.V. omit pas
72. D.P.V. omit sgo
73. D.P.V. spong
74. D.P.V. omit chos kun
75. DN. 'di
76. D.P. omit de nyid
77. D.P.V. omit 'bras bu
78. D.P. phrad
79. D.P. omit 'ang
80. D.P.V. bsgom
81. DN. 'gyur
82. D.P.V. omit chos rnams; D.P. bzhin du
83. D.P.V. zhes
84. DN. dmigs
85. D.P. omit spang len
86. D.P. add mi gnas
87. D.P. nas
88. P. brtags
89. D.P.V. add med de
90. V. shes
91. D.P.DN. bar
92. DN. gyi
93. D. goms, P.V. bsgoms
94. D.P.V. add bsgoms pas

95. M.
96. D.P.V. add chen po
97. D.P. bstan
98. D.P. skyed
99. V. bsgoms; D.P. add pa'i gnas
100. D.P.V. omit rnam grol
101. DN. sgom pa
102. V. pas
103. D.P. chen po
104. V. byas
105. D. yis
106. DN.V. rgyal bas
107. V. dpa'i
108. D.P.V. omit rnams kyi
109. D.P. omit 'ang
110. DN. min
111. D.P.V. add tsam du
112. DN. dang ba'i
113. D. gsung, P. bsrungs
114. D.P. srungs
115. D.P.V. omit gal te
116. D.P.V.de
117. D. chugs, P.V. chungs
118. V. reads rgyal ba sangs rgyas
119. D.P.V. add las
120. D.P.V. omit skye dang
121. D.P.V. ba
122. V. rtogs
123. V. rtogs
124. D.P.DN. ldog
125. V.DN. add pa
126. V.DN. gis
127. D. lam, P.V. yis
128. D.P.V. bden pa
129. V. la
130. D.P.V. spong
131. DN. omit thugs rjer rung zhing thugs rje'i
132. DN.V. 'o 'phrogs
133. D. nyid gu
134. D.P.V. bdud rtsi

135. D.P.V. omit lam mchog
136. D.P. omit dam pa
137. D.N. omit thugs kyi
138. DN. add nyid las
139. D.P.V. read rab bgyis pas
140. D.P. ba'i
141. DN. omits this line
142. V.DN. 'dir
143. only DN.

APPENDIX 2

The Topical Outline (*Sa bcad*) of the *Theg pa gcod pa'i 'khor lo*[1]

NOTES

FOREWORD

1. On this term see *bSam gtan mig sgron* (Leh, Ladakh: 'Khor gdon gter sprul 'Chi med rig 'dzin, 1974), pp. 369–375. A hypersphere is a sphere in a hypothetical multidimensional space, often made use of in modern cosmological theories. Another term useful in this regard is *isotropic*, "the same in all directions." Modern cosmology has concluded that the large-scale distribution of matter in the universe is isotropic.

2. See *bSam gtan mig sgron*, pp. 320–328.

3. Ibid., pp. 328–340

4. See Introduction, Section I.

5. See Introduction, Section I, note 19.

6. Ibid.

7. See Introduction, Section I, note 6.

8. On these three, see H. V. Guenther, *Kindly Bent to Ease Us*, Part I: Mind (Emeryville, Calif.: Dharma Press, 1976), index.

9. See Text note 1.

10. See *Kindly Bent to Ease Us*, chap. 8, and Guenther, *The Jewel Ornament of Liberation* (Boston: Shambhala Publications, 1986), chap. 10.

11. See pp. xiii–xiv.

12. *nges pa lnga*: teacher, message, audience, place, time. See Guenther, *Buddhist Philosophy in Theory and Practice* (Baltimore: Penguin Books, 1972), p. 185.

13. Ibid., pp. 157–158.

14. See Introduction, Section II, note 20.

15. *rgyal ba dgongs brgyud*. See Introduction, Section I, note 8.

16. *brda'i brgyud*. Ibid.

17. *snyan brgyud*. Ibid.

18. *rig 'dzin pho mo*.

19. See Guenther, *Kindly Bent to Ease Us*, index.

20. See Introduction, Section I.

21. See Introduction, Section I, note 25.

PREFACE

1. George Steiner has noted this phenomena in regard to translations of Chinese literature, although we are less positive about it in regard to translations of Buddhist literature. He states:

> Erroneously or not, by virtue of initial chance or of method, the Western eye has fixed on certain constants—or what are taken to be constants—of Chinese landscape, attitude, and emotional register. Each translation in turn appears to corroborate what is fundamentally a Western "invention of China." (*After Babel* [Oxford; Oxford University Press, 1977] p. 359)

He sums up his point as follows: "The more remote the linguistic-cultural source, the easier it is to achieve a summary penetration and a transfer of stylized, codified markers" (p. 361). It is this homogeneity of tone which characterizes most translations of Buddhist texts, in the form of the creation of "stylized, codified markers", i.e., a Buddhist tribal language of translation. What is absent in this uniformity is what Steiner refers to as "semantic specificity" and "particularity of context." In part, this is excusable, given the nascent state of Tibetan studies in the West; in part it is due to a lack of sophistication (i.e., training) in matters of translation among Asian scholars.

2. See p. 70.

3. *Primordial contact* is a term borrowed from Samuel Mallin's excellent exegesis of Merleau-Ponty's philosophy. See his *Merleau-Ponty's Philosophy* (New Haven: Yale University Press, 1979), chap. 2.1. Of course, knowing this is not necessary to appreciate "primordial contact"; neither is its usage here anachronistic, for its usage here bends or skews the precise meaning the form has in Merleau-Ponty's philosophy.

4. *The Tibetan Book of the Dead*, tr. Trungpa and Fremantle (Berkeley: Shambhala Publications, 1975), p. 52.

5. M. Merleau-Ponty, *The Phenomenology of Perception* (London: Routledge & Kegan Paul, 1978), p. 179, n. 1.

6. Ibid., p. 184

7. This is one of the four "reliances" (*rton pa, pratisarana*) or basic principles of Buddhist "hermeneutics": rely on the teaching or message (*dharma, chos*) rather than the personality (*gang zag, pudgala*) of the teacher; rely on the meaning or intent (*don, ārtha*) rather than on the mere words (*tshig*, vyañjana) of a teaching; rely on primordial, ever-fresh awareness (*ye shes, jñāna*) rather than on ordinary, judgmental awareness (*rnam shes, vijñāna*); and finally, rely on teachings whose meaning is definitive (*nges don, nītārtha*) rather than provisional (*drang don, neyārtha*). Cf. *L'Abhidharmakośa de Vasubandhu*, tr. L. de la Vallée Poussin (Paris: Paul Geunther, 1925), chap. 9, pp. 246–247; K. Lipman, "*Nītārtha, Neyārtha*, and *Tathāgatagarbha* in Tibet," *Journal of Indian Philosophy* 8 (1980), pp. 87–95, especially n. 2; *Kongtrul's*

Encyclopedia of Indo-Tibetan Culture, ed. Lokesh Chandra (New Delhi, 1970), Part III, pp. 11–14.

8. P. Ricoeur, "Human Science and Hermeneutical Method," in D. Carr and E. Casey, eds., *Explorations in Phenomenology* (The Hague: Nijhoff, 1973), p. 42.

9. For an excellent critique of the "letter versus spirit" dichotomy in the history of translation, see Steiner, pp. 251–278.

10. See, for example, R. A. Stein, *Vie et chants de 'Brugs pa Kun legs, le yogin* (Paris: G.-P. Maisonneuve et Larose, 1972), p. 32.

11. *gDams ngag mdzod*, compiled by 'Jam mgon Kong sprul Blo-gros mtha'-yas (Delhi: N. Lungtok & N. Gyaltsan, 1971), p. 271.

12. See, for example, Jam mgon 'Ju Mi pham rgya mtsho, *mKhas pa'i tshul la 'jug pa'i sgo* (Ka sbug [Kalimpong]: gSung rab nyams gso rgyun spel bar khang, 1963), fol. 11a.

13. Eugene Gendlin, a psychologist at the University of Chicago, has spent many years exploring the phenomenology of how we "language" our experience, and has developed a practice, which he calls focusing, to help make this "languaging" more precise and satisfying. See, for example, his "Experiential Phenomenology" in M. Natanson, ed., *Phenomenology and the Social Sciences* (Evanston: Northwestern University Press, 1973), pp. 281–319, as well as his *Focusing* (New York: Bantam Books, 1981).

14. D. S. Ruegg has touched on this problem in his excellent review of H. V. Guenther's translation of *The Jewel Ornament of Liberation*, "A Propos of a Recent Contribution to Tibetan and Buddhist Studies," *Journal of the American Oriental Society*, 1963, p. 328ff.

15. See p. 13.

16. Alex Wayman, *Calming the Mind and Discerning the Real* (New York: Columbia University Press, 1978), p. 486, etc.; Robert Thurman, *The Holy Teaching of Vimalakīrti* (University Park, Pa.; Pennsylvania State University Press, 1976), p. 174. *Zung-'grel, yuganaddha*, refers to an indivisible unity; *ngan-song, durgati*, refers to the three undesirable states of existence, that of animals, pretas, and hell-beings.

17. Merleau-Ponty, p. 187.

A NOTE

1. Other areas of scholarship learned Mr. Pound's lesson better, as names like David and Marjorie Grene, Richmond Lattimore, Burton Watson, and many, many more all testify.

2. The details are in *The Letters of Ezra Pound*, D. H. Paige, ed. (New York: Harcourt, Brace, 1950).

3. This term is translated in the course of the present volume. Here it may be understood as "One who has awakened and responded to what is," or more simply, an "Awakened One."

INTRODUCTION

SECTION I

1. On Mañjuśrīmitra's works, see R. N. Davidson, "The Litany of Names of Mañjuśrī," in *Tantric and Taoist Studies in Honor of R. A. Stein*, ed. M. Strickmann (Brussels: Institut Belge des Hautes Études Chinoises, 1981), Mélanges Chinoises et Bouddhique, vol. 20. There is also the tradition that there was a second Mañjuśrīmitra who was a teacher of Padmasambhava, 125 years after the first, according to the *mKhas pa'i dga' ston* of dPa' bo gtsug lag, ed. Lokesh Chandra (New Delhi: International Academy of Indian Culture, 1959), Part I, p. 204. 'Jigs med gling pa's *dkar chag* to the *rNying ma rgyud 'bum* (hereafter *NGB*) contains the cryptic utterance: "byang chub sems sgom rdo la gser zhun med/yang byang chub kyi sems sgom 'jam dpal bshes gnyen phyi ma'i man ngag." (quoted in Kaneko, Eiichi, *Kotantora zenshu kai mokuroku* [A Complete Catalog of the rNying ma rgyud 'bum] [Tokyo: Kokusho Kangyokai, 1982], p. 16). This statement only makes sense upon consulting Tshe dbang mchog grub's accompanying *rNying rgyud 'bum rtogs brjod*, which reads: "byang chub sems bsgom pa rdo la gser zhun *le'u* med pa 'gyur byang ma 'khod pa." (emphasis added) in *rNying ma rgyud 'bum* (Thimbu, Bhutan, 1973), vol. 36, p. 505. That is, our text is without any chapter headings, while there is another recension with chapter divisions (see below, note 17). The second sentence of the first quotation above probably refers to another text of the same name by the second Mañjuśrīmitra.

2. *'Dus pa mdo dbang gi bla ma brgyud pa'i rnam thar ngo mtshar dad pa'i phreng ba* (Leh, Ladakh: S. W. Tashigangpa, 1972), p. 82.

3. See, for example, *Thig-le kun gsal chen po'i rgyud*, in *NGB*, vol. 5, p. 289; *Lo rgyus chen mo* in *Bi ma snying thig* (New Delhi: Trulku Tsewang, Jamyang, and L. Tashi, 1970), Part III, p. 104, where the names of Mañjuśrīmitra's parents differ from the account we translate here, and the events are placed 544 years after the *parinirvāna* of Śākyamuni; *Lo rgyus rin po che'i phreng ba* in *Bla ma yang thig*, Part E, pp. 18–19; *Chos byung me tog snying po sbrang rtsi'i bcud* of Nyang ral nyi ma'i 'od zer, Manuscript B (Paro, Bhutan: Ugyen Tenpai Gyaltsen, 1979), *Rin chen gter mdzod chen po'o rgyab chos*, v. 6, p. 578; Keneko, pp. 34, 123.

4. The five are *bzo rig*, arts and crafts; *gso rig*, medicine; *sgra rig*, poetics and grammar; *tshad ma'am gtan tshigs gi rig*, logic; and *nang don gi rig*, Buddhist philosophy.

5. *Bai ro tsa na'i rnam thar dra 'bag chen mo* in *Vairocana rgyud 'bum* (hereafter *VGB*) (Leh, Ladakh: T. Y. Tashigangpa, 1971), pp. 439–440. There is also the edition of Khams smyon Dharma Senge (Dehra Dun: D. G. Khochen Tulku, n.d.), p. 44ff.

6. See, for example, G. Tucci, *The Religions of Tibet* (London: Routledge & Kegan Paul, 1980), p. 76ff.; H. V. Guenther, *Buddhist Philosophy in Theory and Practice* (Baltimore: Penguin Books, 1971), chaps. 7 and 8.

7. See Foreword by N. Norbu, above.

8. This refers to a means of instruction whereby the teacher shows an object, or performs an act of symbolic significance (*brda*) for a disciple spiritually ripe to understand it. See, for example, the famous case of Tilopa and Naropa in H. V. Guenther, *The Life and Teaching of Naropa* (Oxford: Oxford University Press, 1963), p. 38ff. In the rDzogs chen tradition this type of transmission is known as the *rig 'dzin brda'i brgyud*, on which see, for example, E. M. Dargyay, *The Rise of Esoteric Buddhism in Tibet* (Delhi: Motilal Banarsidass, 1976), p. 14ff., and Foreword by N. Norbu, above.

9. See Kaneko, pp. 31–32. This is a traditional reference to the totality of the rDzogs chen teachings; it was said that Mañjuśrīmitra first made the classification into the three *sde* (*Lo rgyus chen mo*, p. 104).

10. Yamāntaka (gshin rje gshed) is the wrathful form of Mañjuśrī.

11. *Dra 'bag chen mo*, pp. 441–442.

12. *bsTan 'gyur*, Peking ed. 5841, v. 144, pp. 115–122.

13. *mKhas pa'i dga' ston*, Part I, p. 221.

14. Verses: P. 3418, v. 75, pp. 247–250; Tōhōku (hereafter *T*) 2591, sde sge rgyud, v. cu, f. 1b–4b; *VGB*, vol. 5, f. 314–327; *gDams ngag mdzod* (Delhi: N. Lungtok and N. Gyaltsen, 1971), v. 1, pp. 203–212. Commentary: P. 3405, v. 75, pp. 140–147; T. 2578, rgyud, v. ngu f. 45b–59a; *VGB*, vol. 5, pp. 269–303 (incomplete).

15. *VGB*, v. 5, pp. 1–59. For a structural outline (*sa bcad*) of this text, see Appendix 2.

16. *Collected Writings* (Gangtok, Sikkim: Sonam Kazi, 1976), v. 12, p. 465.

17. NGB, v. 3, pp. 88–108. This work contains the following verses of our text: ch. 1, v. 2; ch. 3, vv. 3–17, 18–26; ch. 7, vv. 27–59, 60–78; ch. 8, vv. 79–100, 102–102, 104–110; ch. 9, vv. 109–113; ch. 10, vv. 114–141; ch. 11, vv. 142–147.

18. An exception is Sog bzlog pa blo gros rgyal mtshan, *bDag po rin po che'i chos 'byung la zhal snga nas blo bzang pos dgag pa mdzad* in his *Collected Works* (New Delhi: Sanje Dorje, 1975), V. II, pp. 257–258, where he holds that our text is not one of the *snga 'gyur lnga* but one of the eighty-two *sems phran*, or minor works of the *sems sde*.

19. =*kun 'byed rgyal po*, ch. 31, *nyi zla dang mnyam pa dri ma med pa'i rgyud*, ch. 2 (see Kaneko, pp. 3, 9). A commentary on this work exists among the Tun Huang documents. See L. de la Vallée Poussin, *Catalog of the Tibetan Manuscripts from Tun Huang in the India Office Library* (Oxford: Oxford University Press, 1962), p. 206, n. 647. Professor Norbu and I have prepared a translation and study of this work that we plan to publish.

20. Klong chen pa dri med 'od zer, *Chos dbyings rin po che'i mdzod 'grel pa* (Gangtok, Sikkim: Dodrup Chen Rinpoche), p. 206b.

21. No. 19 (*Kaneko, no.* 1) is the principal *tantra* of the *sems sde*. For a translation of Klong chen pa's summary of this text, see K. Lipman and M. Peterson, *You Are the Eyes of the World* (Snow Lion, 2000).

22. These are *thos pa'i shes rab*, through listening, i.e., studying; *bsam pa'i shes rab*, through thinking about what one has studied; and *sgom pa'i shes rab*, cultivating a direct experience of what one has thought about.

23. These represent the state of the individual's body (*lus*), speech (*ngag*), and mind (*yid*) at the level of goal realization, at which time one may speak about primordial contact (*sku*), communication (*gsung*), and experiencing (*thugs*). See H. V. Guenther, *Tibetan Buddhism in Western Perspective* (Emeryville, Calif.: Dharma Press, 1977), pp. 84, 105, 127; and our Preface above.

24. *mKhas pa'i dga' ston*, I, p. 221. dPa' bo gtsug lag lists only seventeen works, and the eighteenth text in Klong chen pa's list is the only one which does not tally with the former's list, nor have I been able to identify it.

25. *Chos 'byung*, p. 510.

26. *bSam gtan mig sgron* (Leh, Ladakh: 'Khor gdon gter sprul 'Chi med rig 'dzin, 1974), ch. 7, p. 296, etc.

27. *bSam gtan mig sgron*, p. 316ff.

28. *VGB*, v. 2, pp. 41–55; Kaneko, no. 7, p. 10. The other three *tantras* are nos. 4–6 in Kaneko.

29. The commentary by dGa' rab rdo rje is P. 2942, v. 67, pp. 251–262; Vimalamitra's is P. 2941, v. 67, pp. 233–251.

30. P. 3389, v. 75, 130, 2, 6–7.

31. *mudrā* (*phyag rgya*). On the four *mudrās*, although in a different tradition, see H. V. Guenther, *The Tantric View of Life* (Berkeley: Shambhala Publications, 1972), p. 57ff. There are various orderings for the *mudrās*; for their meaning in the context of Mahāyoga, see Rong zom chos kyi bzang po, *Man ngag lta phreng 'grel*, in *Selected Writings* (Leh, Ladakh: 'Khor gdon gter sprul 'Chi med rig 'dzin, 1974), pp. 84–85.

32. See p. 106. On the three contemplations, see Rong zom, p. 88. They relate to what is usually called the "stage of generation" (*bskyed rim*).

SECTION II

1. Although a distinction can be made between *Yogācāra* and *Cittamātra*, as nonreductionist and reductionist systems, respectively, this is not necessary for our purposes here and would only complicate matters unduly.

2. See p. 78.

3. See p. 82.

4. P. 5557. This text is the basis for the celebrated Chinese commentary, the *Vijñaptimātratāsiddhi* (*Ch'eng Wei Shih Lun*), compiled by Hsuan Tsang. See Poussin, tr. (Paris: Paul Geuthner, 1928).

5. See p. 83.

6. See Lipman, K., "The Cittamātra and Its Madhyamaka Critique: Some

Phenomenological Reflections," *Philosophy East and West*, 32, no. 3 (July 1982), p. 298, for this understanding of *ālayavijñāna*.

7. E. Husserl has made a distinction in his phenomenology between intentionality as an act (which would correspond to the *kliṣṭomanovijñāna*) and an anonymously functioning intentionality, which "founds" the "ego-act," but he did not develop this insight. It was left to Merleau-Ponty to make this a central theme of his phenomenology of perception. See G. Brand, "Intentionality, Reduction, and Intentional Analysis in Husserl's Later Manuscripts," in J. Kockelmans, ed., *Phenomenology* (Garden City, N.Y.: Doubleday, 1967), p. 197ff.

8. See p. 87.

9. See p. 87.

10. This topic is succinctly discussed in the least known of the so-called "Five Treatises of Maitreya" (*Byams chos sde lnga*), the *Dharmadharmatāvibhāga* (*Chos dang chos nyid rnam 'byed*). Buddhist cosmology speaks of two realms, that of sentient beings and of the environments that they inhabit. In the *Dharmadharmatāvibhāga*, the realm of beings is divided into public and private domains (*thun mong, thun mong ma yin*). Both of these domains, as well as the environment (which may be called "wholly public" for clarity's sake), are not to be found apart from "experiencing" (*citta, sems*). In more modern parlance, one would speak of the "social construction of reality" or "intersubjectivity." Mipham rgya mtsho, commenting on the statement in the *Dharmadharmatāvibhāga* about the public aspect of intersubjectivity (section VII, 5 in the edition of Yamaguchi-Nozawa, "The Dharmadharmatāvibhāga and -vrtti," in *Studies in Indology and Buddhology Presented in Honor of Professor Susumu Yamaguchi's 60th Birthday* (Kyoto: Hozokan, 1955), says:

> As to what is apparently real (*chos*), there is in the domain of sentient beings, that which is public as well as that which is private. . . . What is public in the domain of sentient beings is: birth from a womb; conventional vocally and bodily conveyed information; exchanges between individuals; fighting; aiding; harming; the arising of positive qualities, such as educatedness, and of faults, such as attachment, through being influenced by another. In these cases, since the arising of a perception of something which appears public, functions as a mutually motivating factor (*phan tshun rgyu byed pa*) by becoming the predominant condition (*bdag pa'i rkyen*) operating between sentient beings, it is called "that which is present publicly." In this regard, the way in which birth is in the realm of public, commonly shared experiences, is that by one's own karma as impetus along with the common impetus of the simultaneously operating contributory condition (*lhan cig byed rkyen*) coming from the generative capacities of the father and mother, the body of a person is born from a womb

as a result. The publicness of convention is, for example, understanding the words and viewpoint of another, having been influenced by their vocally and bodily conveyed information. In the same way, mutually exchanging goods or information; killing through quarrels, armies, and the like; providing what is useful through protection from harm, etc.; harming by striking, etc.; generating positive qualities through education, etc.; and engaging in activities which are faulty since they generate attachment and teach wrongheaded points of view: all these have as the dominant condition for their arising another individual who is the primary factor in causing a (mental or physical) event in oneself. These are called "public" in their aspect of establishing a single, public result. Although, conventionally speaking, by the assemblage of such causes and conditions, corresponding results are to be found, however, in reality, what is called the "dominant cause," i.e., an independently existing object or state of affairs as an objective condition apart from an information-providing awareness (*rnam par rig pa*, *vijñāpti*), is not to be found if enquired into.

Further, since that which appears as wholly public, such as the outer environment, also doesn't exist apart from being merely the apprehendable aspect (*gzung cha*) of an internal, information-providing awareness, a public thing-in-itself is thereby demonstrated not to be found if inquired into. (*Chos dang chos nyid rnam par 'byed pa'i tshig le'ur byas pa'i 'grel pa ye shes snang ba rnam 'byed*, in *Collected Writings*, v. 3, pp. 620–621.)

11. *Phenomenology of Perception* (London: Routledge & Kegan Paul, 1962), p. 184.

12. Ibid., p. 352.

13. See S. Levi, *Vijñaptimātratāsiddhi* (Paris: Librairie Ancienne Honoré Champion, 1925), p. 15, and *Sthiramati's Triṁśikābhāsyam, A Tibetan Text*, Enga, Teramoto, ed. (Kyoto: Otani Daigaku, 1933), p. 1.

14. P. 5571, v. 114, 175, 3, 1.

15. Teramoto, p. 3; Levi, p. 16.

16. See his *Vigrahavyāvartanī*, translated in, for example, F. J. Streng, *Emptiness: A Study in Religious Meaning* (New York: Abingdon Press, 1967).

17. Quoted in K. Lipman "A Controversial Topic from Mi-pham's Analysis of Sāntarakṣita's *Madhyamakālamkāra*," in *Windhorse I*, Proceedings of the North American Tibetological Society (Berkeley: Asian Humanities Press, 1981), pp. 45–46, to be reprinted together with *Windhorse II*, in press.

18. See p. 92.

19. The point to be developed here is how the *sems sde* encompasses the sutric Yogācāra approach. Unfortunately, another lengthy introduction

would be required to discuss the relation of rDzogs chen to the Madhyamaka. To put it simply: just as rDzogs chen encompasses the *Cittamatra* (*sems tsam pa*) by understanding that *citta* (*sems*) is the "creativity" or "excitement" of *bodhicitta* (byang chub sems) or *rig pa*, it also encompasses the Madhyamaka by understanding *śūnyatā* (*stong pa nyid*) as a facet of *rig pa*. 'Jigs med gling pa states succintly in his *sNying thig sgom pa'i bya bral gyi gol shor tshar gcod senge nga ro*:

> Openness refers to the flash of knowing which gives awareness its quality, present right now beyond the realm of intellect. It is primordially, radically open, has nothing about it which makes it what it is, and is free from the four or eight limitations elaborated by the intellect. Not understanding this, in the lower vehicles one asserts an openness which is a mere nothing in the wake of an intellectual analysis that affirms and denies the existence and nonexistence (of entities).

(*Klong chen snying thig*, v. III [Paro, Bhutan: Ngodrub and Shesrab Drimay, 1978], *Rin chen gter mdzod chen mo*, v. 108, p. 564)

All this discussion is part of the larger issue of the "four distinguishing superiorities" of Tantrism (*khyad par 'phags pa bzhi*) in regard to the *sūtras*. On this see H. V. Guenther, *Buddhist Philosophy in Theory and Practice*, chap. 6. The locus classicus for the four superiorities is the *Nayatrayapradīpa*, P. 4530, v. 81. See also below, note 34.

20. In his translation of dPal sprul's commentary on the *Tshig gsum gnad brdegs* of dGa' rab rdo rje (*The Three Incisive Precepts of Garab Dorje* [Kathmandu: Diamond Sow Publications, 1982], p. 4), K. Dowman makes the remark that *rtsal* has connotations of "masculine potency" and *rol pa* that of "feminine fecundity." This brings up the fascinating question of the relationship of rDzogs chen to the later Hinduistic theistic schools that developed in reaction to Śaṅkara's Advaita, especially Śaivite Tantrism, but we can only broach the question here. rDzogs chen has been attacked explicitly for being Sāṃkhya doctrine in disguise (it is the Sāṃkhya which provides the metaphysical background for Śaivite theism, for example). On this see, for example, S. Karmay, "A Discussion on the Doctrinal Position of rDzogs chen from the 10th to the 13th Centuries," *Journal Asiatique* 263 (1975), pp. 147–155.

21. These are from *Mahāyānasūtrālaṃkāra*, XI, 40.

22. *Yid bzhin rin po che'i mdzod kyi 'grel pa padma dkar po* (Gangtok, Sikkim: Dodrup Chen Rinpoche), pp. 17–18.

23. This is probably the massive *Thig le kun gsal chen po'i rgyud* in 97 chapters. See Kaneko, no. 81.

24. *Grub mtha' rin po che'i mdzod* (Gangtok, Sikkim: Dodrup Chen Rinpoche), pp. 333–334.

25. On the eight similes, see H. V. Guenther, *Kindly Bent to Ease Us, Part Three: Wonderment* (Emeryville, Calif.: Dharma Press, 1976).

26. These arguments are presented more at length in the *Yid bzhin mdzod*.

See K. Lipman, "How the Saṃsāra Is Fabricated from the Ground of Being," *Crystal Mirror*, v. 5, 1977, pp. 353–354.

27. *rNying ma rgyud 'bum bcu bdun* (New Delhi: Sanje Dorje, 1977), v. 1, p. 256, reads: "cir snang sems su 'dod pa nga la sgrib pa yin." Klong chen pa quotes this as "snang ba sems su 'dod pa nga las gol ba yin." He was probably quoting from memory, since we know that he spent many of his creative years wandering homelessly with his teacher, Kumararaja.

28. Ibid., pp. 734, 736. The material in brackets has been supplied from the original text to make the quotation intelligible.

29. The eight modes of awareness are the eight *vijñāna* of the Yogācāra discussed above. The three life-worlds are those of desire, form, and formlessness.

30. That is, *bodhicitta* is a term that uses the word, *bodhi*, a name for the goal, although it itself refers to the starting point.

31. *gNas lugs rin po che'i mdzod* (Gangtok, Sikkim: Dodrup Chen Rinpoche), pp. 49–52. This is as close to a definition of terms like *rtsal* and *rol pa* as one will find in the literature. In the *gZhi khregs chod skabs kyi zin bris bstan pa'i nyi ma'i zhal lung snyan brgyud chu bo'i bcud dus* (Dehru Dun: sPom mda' mkhan po, 1963 or 1964), which consists of notes by mKhan po ngag dbang dpal bzang (1871–1941) on talks by the Third Do grub chen, 'Jigs med bstan pa'i nyi ma, the *Sems sde* is presented making use of *rtsal, rol pa,* and *rgyan* in the following way:

> In the *sems sde* approach, how things appear is to be understood as experience (*snang ba sems su ngo sprod*); experience is then to be understood as open (*sems stong par ngo sprod*); openness is then to be understood as the flash of knowing which gives awareness its quality (*stong pa rig par ngo sprod*); and then openness and the flash of knowing are to be understood as a unity (*rig stong zun 'jug tu ngo sprod*). The understanding that, "how things appear is experience" is accomplished through the triad of creativity, excitement and adornment. First, how creativity works, is that the bare movement (*'gyu tsam*) and mere flash of knowing, which are the natural creativity of the primordial capacity of awareness (*ye shes*), become a basis upon which the fundamental structure of experience is founded. This structure has error built right into it. From that, the arising of the emotionally perturbed ego-centered awareness, the five forms of sensory awareness, and so forth, are the energy of excitement. From that, the display of the bodies of beings and their environments, mountains, houses, and so forth, internally and externally, is what is called the energy of adornment. In short, adornment and excitement arise from this pure movement and flash of knowing, which are themselves the energy of creativity, and that also comes from the unique fact of awareness, which is like an

all-creating king (*kun 'byed rgyal po*). Thus, it is in this sense
that how things appear is to be understood as just experience.
(f. 6a–b)
Once again, one should note here the extensive use of Yogācāra terminology.

32. *rdol thabs*, the method of "letting whatever happens, happen." See
Introduction, Section III, p. 31.

33. This seems to be a reference to the process of falling asleep, in which, as
in the *bar do*, there is a state of "natural luminosity" where *rig pa*
shines forth, before the phase of dreaming begins.

34. This passage complements the discussion from the *Yid bzhin mdzod*
translated above (pp. 20–21), where Klong chen pa criticizes those
followers of the Cittamātra line of thought who do not understand the
distinction between how things appear (*snang ba*) and that which
appears (*snang yul*). As mentioned above, this distinction is implicit in
Cittamātra thought; how things appear is "mental" while that which
appears, mountains and trees, are not. Logically, one is then led to ask:
from where does this distinction itself arise? Is it to be understood
realistically, or as just a product of "mind"? Yogācāra philosophy has
no other strategy than to answer with the latter alternative, but "mind"
is one of the terms of the distinction we are trying to account for.
Further, according to its own method, this answer only explains how
we take things (*snang ba sems yin*), but not the fact that there are things
for us (which, we have seen, cannot be accounted for within the context
of realism, either).
   The rDzogs chen approach explains this duality as the "energy" of
the primordial state of the individual (*byang chub sems*). By merely
analyzing the mistaken way in which we experience things, the onto-
logical mystery of there being "things" and "minds" can only be very
obliquely addressed. This is not to say that Yogācāra thought is incor-
rect or even deficient; it is fully suited to its strategy of deconstructing
our mistaken way of taking things. Once again, this argument forms
part of the "four superiorities of Tantrism," specifically the first, the
way in which Tantrism is not at all confused (*mi rmongs pa*) about the
methods for goal realization. See, for example, bSod nams rtse mo,
rGyud sde phyi'i rnam bzhag, in *Sa skya bka' 'bum*, bSod nams rgya
mtsho, ed. (Tokyo: Toyo Bunko, 1968), v. 2, f. 17a; *Grub mtha'
mdzod*, p. 258. Tsong kha pa's attitude is to be found in *Tantra in
Tibet*, tr. J. Hopkins (London: George Allen and Unwin, 1977), p. 145ff.
It is not clear, however, in the presentation there whether it is just
Tripiṭakamāla's (the author of the *Nayatryapradīpa*) interpretation of
the four superiorities that is being rejected, or the whole schema.

35. *Chos dbyings rin po che'i mdzod*, ff. 71b–72b.

36. See Foreword by N. Norbu.

SECTION III

1. The text is found in VGB, v. 1, ff. 49–64. The scribal errors in the VGB are atrocious. Unfortunately no other edition has been published to date.

2. See Guenther, *Life and Teaching of Nāropa*, p. 115.

3. For an extremely lucid presentation of the four *rnal 'byor* and the *sems sde* in general, see *Kaḥ thog pa nam mkha' rdo rje, Slob dpon dga' rab rdo rje nas brgyud pa'i rdzogs pa chen po sems sde'i phra khrid kyi man ngag*, in *gDams ngag mdzod*, vol. 1, pp. 305–355 (hereafter *phra khrid*). Pp. 317 and 318 of this edition are actually a reprinting of pp. 199 and 200.

4. In his *bSam gtan mig sgron*, gNubs chen sangs rgyas ye shes uses a very strong example in this regard: even the meditation of the *cig car ba* ("all-at-once") approach of the Ch'an school is like a duck trying to stir up the ocean. Quoted in Guenther, "Meditation Trends in Early Tibet," in L. Lancaster and W. Lai, eds., *Early Ch'an in China and Tibet* (Berkeley: Berkeley Buddhist Studies Series, 1983), p. 358.

5. In the *sems sde*, first *zhi gnas* and then *lhag mthong* are practiced. In the *klong sde* and *man ngag sde*, the practitioner enters the state of pure and total presence through the exercise of the four *brda* ("indicators") in the former, and the four *cog bzhag* ("letting be") of the *khregs chod* in the latter. A very clear and simple presentation of the *klong sde* meditation is to be found in the *rDzogs pa chen po klong sde'i snyan brgyud rin po che rdo rje zam pa'i sgom khrid kyi lag len*, in *gDams ngag mdzod*, v. 1 pp. 408–416. The literature on the practices of the *man ngag sde* or *snying thig*, which comprise many *gter ma*, is enormous. Their core, however, are the practices of the *khregs chod* and the *thod rgal*. One of the most straightforward presentations of these we have seen is the *bTags grol snying po'i don khrid* of the *mKha' 'gro snying thig*, in the *sNying thig ya bzhi* (New Delhi: Trulku Tsewang, Jamyang, and L. Tashi, 1970), v. 2, pp. 82–106.

6. See p. 37.

7. "Speech" in this triad refers to all the subtle bodily energies linked up with the use of the voice and breathing, summed up by the intuitive term *prāna (rlung)*.

8. Cf. H. V. Guenther, *Kindly Bent to Ease Us*, Part Two: Meditation (Emeryville, Calif.: Dharma Press, 1976), pp. 32–36 and chap. 3.

9. See pp. 37–38.

10. These are *śūnyatā* (openness), *ānimitta* (absence of identifying characteristics), and *apraṇihita* (absence of wishfulness). See E. Conze, *Buddhist Thought in India* (Ann Arbor: University of Michigan Press, 1967), pp. 59–69.

11. *rang rig pa'i mngon sum*. This term is borrowed from the Buddhist logicians, for whom, there are four valid means of knowledge (*mngon sum, pratyakṣa*): sensory knowledge (*dbang po'i mngon sum, indriya-*

pratyaksa), mental knowledge (*yid kyi mngon sum, mānasapratyaksa*), nonreferential knowledge (rang rig pa'i mngon sum, *svasaṃvedanapratyaksa*), and yogic knowledge (*rnal 'byor shes pa'i mngon sum, yogijñānapratyakṣa*). "Nonreferential knowledge" means, for the logicians, that, in all acts of knowing one is immediately, nonreferentially aware of one's own state (without it being a propositional knowledge of oneself as "subject"). Such a knowledge, of course, is still within the domain of "mind"; it presents a useful analogy to *rig pa* as understood in rDzogs chen.

12. *Byang chub sems bsgom pa'i rgyud*. We have not been able to locate this *tantra*. It is not the text mentioned above in Section I, note 17.

13. See *phra khrid*, pp. 322ff., 334ff.

14. Often three types of self-liberation are discussed: the first is that thoughts are freed into their own dimension (the *dharmakāya*) as if one were meeting an old friend; the second is that they are freed like a snake unwinding itself (the point being that less mental effort is involved here than in the first example, where one has to observe and recognize one's old friend); and the third, which is the most fully developed form, is that thoughts are like thieves who come to an empty house. See, for example, dPal sprul o rgyan chos kyi dbang po, *mKhas pa sri rgyal po'i khyad chos*, ff. 10b–11a (pp. 17–18 in K. Dowman, tr., *The Three Incisive Precepts of Garab Dorje*). Here, dPal sprul makes the extremely important point that, for someone skilled in self-liberation of thought, thoughts arise as they did before, as is the case with ordinary people; one experiences hope and fear, pain and pleasure. But the crucial difference is that the ordinary person, through judging these thought processes either affirmatively (acceptance) or negatively (rejection), becomes caught up in situations, one after another, and thus becomes conditioned by his or her own self-generated attachment and/or aversion to these thought-situations.

15. This is an interpretation of the ethically positive actions archetypically represented by the *bodhisattva* Samantabhadra (*kun tu bzang po*) eulogized in Mahāyāna liturgy. See pp. 142–143.

16. On "warmth" as a phase of the "linking-up stage" (*sbyor lam*) of the path, see H. V. Guenther, *Philosophy and Psychology in the Abhidharma* (Berkeley: Shambhala Publications, 1976), p. 220, as well as his *Jewel Ornament of Liberation*, chap. 18. On the "indications," see *phra khrid*, pp. 328ff. and 343ff.

17. "Picking out" (*yid la byed pa*, manaskāra) and "attending to" (*dran pa, smṛti*) are specific details of experiencing (*sems byung, caitta*) acutely analyzed in the Abhidharma. See, for example, H. V. Guenther and L. S. Kawamura, *Mind in Buddhist Psychology* (Emeryville, Calif.: Dharma Press, 1975), p. 19ff.

18. On these two often-discussed impediments, see, for example, H. V. Guenther, *Treasures on the Tibetan Middle Way*, chap. 4 and E. Conze, *Buddhist Thought in India*, p. 226.

19. The locus classicus for these five (or four) is the *Mahāyānasūtrālam-kāra*. See Guenther, *Jewel Ornament of Liberation*, p. 258ff. A discussion of how the five *skandhas* are transmuted into the five awarenesses is to be found in Guenther, *The Tantric View of Life*, p. 54ff. A useful chart of these, as well as other correlations involved, is to be found in Guenther, *Buddhist Philosophy in Theory and Practice*, pp. 228–229, n. 12.

20. This is one of the six forms of heightened awareness (*mngon shes, abhi-jñā*). See *Abhidharmakośa* VII, 42, 45.

21. *rdzu 'phrul, rddhi*. See *Abhidharmakośa* VII, 48.

22. See above, Section I, note 10.

THE TEXT

1. A basic device of Buddhist hermeneutics was the distinction between the Buddha's words which dealt with the real meaning and were definitive (*nges don, nītārtha*) and those which were provisional and had a particular intent behind them (*drang don, neyārtha*). On this see K. Lipman, "Nītārtha, Neyārtha and Tathāgatagarbha in Tibet," *Journal of Indian Philosophy* 8 (1980), pp. 87–95, especially note 2.

2. On the ten spiritual levels, see *Jewel Ornament of Liberation*, chap. 19.

3. Ibid., p. 338.

4. In Tibetan, "youthful Mañjuśrī" is *'Jam dpal gzhon nu gyur pa* (Mañ-juśrīkumārabhūta), a combination of "gentle Lord" and "youthful."

5. On the translation of *kāya*, see Preface.

6. The five eyes are those of flesh, of the gods, of discernment (*prajñā*), of the teaching (*dharma*), and of a Buddha. It is the eye of the gods that is able to see future births and deaths.

7. See Introduction, III, note 19.

8. *Vajrasattva* in Tibetan is a compound consisting of *rdo rje* (*vajra*), a symbol of indestructibility, and *sems dpa'* (*sattva*), one who is committed in his or her very being. *Sems dpa'* as a translation of *sattva* is a good example of the principles illustrated in the Preface.

9. See Introduction, III, note 11. In addition to these two well-known *tshad ma*, there is also a group of three used internally among the Buddhists themselves: *lung tshad ma*, authoritative scripture (*āgama*); *rig pa tshad ma*, authoritative experiential knowledge; and *man ngag tshad ma*, authoritative oral instruction (*upadeśa*) of the guru. See, for example, mDo sngags bstan pa'i nyi ma, *lTa grub shan 'byed gnad kyi sgron me yi tshig don rnam bshad 'jam dbyangs dgongs rgyan* (Delhi: mKhas btsun bzang po, 1973), f. 3a, and our translation, p. 113 above.

10. See Section 5 a.ii of our translation.

11. On *mthong lam* (*darśanamārga*), see above, Introduction, Section III, note 19.

12. The five senses and thought.

13. These are the subject matter of the fifth chapter of *The Jewel Ornament of Liberation*.

14. *skye mched (āyatana)*, the six modes of awareness and their respective objects.

15. See Introduction, II.

16. *sems byung (caitta)*, for which see, *Mind in Buddhist Psychology*.

17. See Introduction, II.

18. This traditional antidote to attachment is described in E. Conze, *Buddhist Meditation* (New York: Harper and Row, 1975), p. 103ff.

19. Six schools are traditionally enumerated in groups of two: Nyāya-Vaiśeṣika, Sāṃkhya-Yoga, and Pūrva-Uttaramīmāṃsā (Uttaramīmāṃsā is another name for Vedānta). See S. Dasgupta, *A History of Indian Philosophy*, especially v. 1. The point here is that the *ālayavijñāna* is mistaken for an eternal self.

20. See Introduction, III, note 20.

21. Once again, the critique of Hinduistic thought is based on an experiential lack of understanding of the *ālayavijñāna*. The Madhyamaka, on the other hand, presents a logical critique of a creator, as in, for example, *Madhyamakālaṃkāra*, v. 2, of Śāntarakṣita (P. 5284, v. 101, 1-1-8):

    Since results are gradually produced, these entities which are said to be an eternal (cause) are not of a unitary nature.
    If results are each (produced) gradually (by a variety of causes), the eternality of these (causes) would be destroyed.

22. See above, note 15.

23. Cf. *Madhyamakālaṃkāra*, vv. 79–81 (P. 5289, v. 101, 2-2-4):

    Therefore, in the continuity of beginningless existence, we infer (the existence) of latent tendencies suitable
    To our conceptualizations: concrete entity, abstract entity, and so forth.
    These (concepts) do not arise through the power of concrete entities, since the latter are nonexistent;
    The absolute reality of these concrete entities has been extensively refuted (here).
    Since (what appears) comes about gradually, it is not purely fortuitous, and since neither does it come about all the time, it does not arise from an eternal cause.
    Therefore, on account of a similarity to our latent tendencies, a first (moment of a new experience) is born from that which is similar to itself.

24. On the distinction between pure and impure Buddha-fields, see E. Lamotte, tr., *L'Enseignement de Vimalakīrti* (Louvain: Institute Orientaliste, 1962), pp. 395–404.

25. Cf. E. Conze, *Buddhist Wisdom Books* (New York: Harper and Row,

1972), p. 63, for his translation of the Sanskrit. Our text differs slightly from the Tibetan translation of this *sūtra*, which I have utilized in correcting the text.

26. According to the *Theg pa gcod pa'i 'khor lo*, this line comes under the Mahāyoga refutation of the Madhyamaka. See below, Appendix 2, p. 129, and VGB, v. 5, p. 45. Usually, such a view is ascribed to the Yogācāra logicians who follow Dignāga and Dharmakīrti.

27. According to the *Theg gcod 'khor lo* (VGB, v. 5, p. 45), this refers to the *nirmāṇakāya*.

28. Existence, nonexistence, both, neither.

29. "Lord" is *dbang phyug* in Tibetan, a compound of *dbang*, "powerful," and *phyug*, "rich."

30. The objects of the five senses.

31. See above, note 19.

32. Much emphasis is placed in the *sems sde* on cultivating an awareness of three distinct states: absence of the movement of thoughts (*gnas pa*), especially in the first of the four yogas, *gnas pa'i rnal 'byor*; presence of the movement of thoughts (*'gyu ba*), especially in the second yoga, *mi g.yo ba'i rnal 'byor*; and the pure presence of awareness of these two (*rig pa*). See Introduction, III, note 3, and *phra khrid*.

33. See Introduction, III, note 10.

34. b.iii appears after b.iv, on p. 104.

35. See above, note 4.

36. *dmigs yul*.

37. *rnam par shes pa* (*vijñāna*), "awareness of a perceptible quality."

38. *Arhat* in Tibetan is *dgra bcom pa*, "one who has conquered the enemy," i.e., emotional conflicts.

39. See Introduction, III, note 17.

40. The two are *bsod nams kyi tshogs*, the accumulation of merit, and *ye shes kyi tshogs*, the accumulation of primordial knowledge. The former relates to the relative truth and the practice of compassion; the latter to the absolute truth and the experiential knowledge of openness.

41. On the thirty-seven, see Guenther, *Jewel Ornament of Liberation*, chap. 18; and *Kindly Bent to Ease Us*, Part I, appendix, pp. 341–344. On the ten *pāramitās*, see *Jewel Ornament of Liberation*, chap. 19.

42. On the eight *yon tan* (*guṇa*), see *Uttaratantraśāstra*, I, 5, J. Takasaki, tr., *A Study of the Ratnagotravibhāga* (Roma: ISMEO, 1966), p. 156ff.

43. See Introduction, I, p. 10.

44. See Introduction, I, note 32.

45. On these mudrās, see Introduction, I, note 31. The correlations here are between *sku* (*kāya*) and *phyag rgya chen po* (Mahāmudrā); *thugs* (*citta*) and *dam tshig gi phyag rgya* (*samāyāmudrā*); *phrin las* (karma) and *las kyi phyag rgya* (*karmamudrā*). Cf. Guenther, *Buddhist Philosophy in*

Theory and Practice, p. 189. For a further discussion of *mudrā* in the context of *Mahāyoga*, see the principal *tantra* of the *sgyu 'phrul drwa ba (Māyājāla)* group, the *gSang ba'i snying po de kno na nyid nges pa* (Kaneko, n. 87), chap. 8.

46. The final correlation is betwen *gsung (vāc)* and *chos kyi phyag rgya (dharmamudrā)*. Cf. Guenther, op. cit.

47. Cf. *bSam gtan mig sgron*, p. 194:
    If all configurations of events and meanings are not thoroughly grasped as the state of pure and total presence, which is the flash of knowing that gives awareness its quality, then it presents itself as the variety of concrete bodies and their sufferings. However, if thoroughly grasped, the flash of knowing presents itself as the symbolic encounters with primordial contact, primordial communication, and primordial experience.

48. Samantabhadra *(kun tu bzang po)*, "positive in every way," is masculine, symbolizing skillfulness *(upāya, thabs)*; while Samantabhadrī *(kun tu bzang mo)* is feminine, symbolizing discernment *(prajñā, shes rab)*.

49. The Śrāvakas, although they represent the most limited form of approach to the Buddhist path, are still worthy objects of reverence for beings within the three worlds.

50. *rgyal ba rnam par snang mdzad*, the Buddha Vairocana; here the author is playing on the meaning of *Vairocana*.

51. *maṇḍala, dkyil 'khor*, for which see H. V. Guenther, *Matrix of Mystery* (Boulder: Shambhala Publications, 1984). The supreme commitments *(dam tshig, samāyā)* refer to those connected with *maṇḍala* practice, i.e., the Vajrayāna.

52. *rdo la gser bzhin*; this phrase is the source for the nickname of the text, *rDo la gser zhun*, "Gold Refined from ore."

53. This refers to the tradition that the teaching of Śākyamuni would decline in 500-year stages; see E. Obermiller, tr., *History of Buddhism by Bu-ston* (Tokyo: Suzuki Research Foundation, 1964), Reprint Series no. 5, p. 102ff.

54. See above, note 9.

APPENDIX 2

1. For bibliographic reference, see Introduction, I, note 15.

GLOSSARY OF IMPORTANT
TECHNICAL TERMS

This glossary is intended only as an aid to the reader unfamiliar with our terminology. Other translations are possible, and indeed necessary, in other contexts not found in these texts. Technical terms that occur rarely and are footnoted in the text are not included here. The most important usage is put first. Sanskrit is also given in some cases after the Tibetan.

TIBETAN-ENGLISH

kun gzhi (rnam shes) [ālaya (vijñāna)]	fundamental structuring of all experience
sku [kāya]	primordial contact; dimension; communication
’khrul pa [bhrānti]	deception; deceptive
(ma) grub pa	(not) to be found (if inquired into)
grol	freedom
dgra bcom pa [Arhat]	those who have overcome emotional conflicts
rgyan	"beauty"; enhancement
sgrib pa [āvaraṇa]	impediment
bsgom pa [bhāvanā]	cultivation; meditation
ngang	ongoing(ness)
nges don [nītārtha]	real meaning
ngo bo	what it comes down to; at bottom; in fact
dngos po	entity; concrete(ness)
mngon ’gyur	to make really so; realize

chos sku [dharmakāya]	primordial contact with the total field of events and meanings
chos nyid [dharmatā]	the ultimate content of what is
chos rnams	configurations of events and meanings; phenomena; entities
chos dbyings [dharmadhātu]	total field of events and meanings
nyams	experiential sign of the development of practice
nyon mongs [kleśa]	that which muddies the stream of awareness
mnyam (nyid)	fundamental alikeness; very sameness
snying po	energy pulse; core
ting nge 'dzin [samādhi]	contemplation
rtags	indicator; indicative
rtog pa	grasping of experience through thought; a thought
rtogs	full grasp; thorough comprehension
stong pa (nyid) [śūnyatā]	open(ness); open dimension
brtag pa	inquire into
bstan pa	point out
theg pa chen po [Mahāyāna]	supreme, comprehensive approach
thugs	primordial experience
mtha'	limit; limiting concept; extreme
de bzhin gshegs pa [tāthāgata]	those who have come through
bdag nyid chen po	all-inclusive state of the individual
bdag med [anātman]	there is nothing that makes (anything) what it is
bdud [Māra]	Lord of limitations
'du byed [saṃskāra]	aspects of being caught up in a situation; conditioned events
rdo rje sems dpa'[Vajrasattva]	state of commitment to what is indestructible
rnam shes [vijñāna]	modes of awareness; perception
snang ba	how things appear; appearance; presence; to make itself felt

dpyod pa	think through; think about
pha rol tu phyin pa [pāramitā]	ways of overcoming (limitations)
phyag rgya [mudrā]	"symbolic encounter"
bag chags [vāsanā]	habituating tendencies
byang chub [bodhi]	pure and total presence
byang chub sems [bodhicitta]	the (primordial) state of pure and total presence
byang chub sems dpa' [bodhisattva]	those who are heroically committed to pure and total presence
rtsal	"creativity"
tshad ma [pramāṇa]	valid means of knowing
mtshan nyid [lakṣaṇa]	defining characteristic; by definition
mtshan ma [nimitta]	identifiable characteristic
rdzogs chen	total completeness
ye shes [jñāna]	ever-fresh awareness
rang bzhin [svabhāva]	actuality; essence
rig pa	the flash of knowing that gives awareness its (illumining) quality
rol pa	"excitement"
longs spyod rdzogs pa'i sku [sambhogakāya]	primordial contact with total richness and all its satisfactions
sems [citta]	experiencing; potential for experience; mind; general forms of experience
sems nyid	the unique fact of awareness
sems 'byung [caitta]	specific details of experience
lhug pa	relaxation

ENGLISH-TIBETAN

actuality; essence	rang bzhin
all-inclusive state of the individual	bdag nyid chen po
aspects of being caught up in a situation; conditioned events	'du byed

at bottom; what it comes down . to; in fact	ngo bo
"beauty"; enhancement	rgyan
configurations of events and meanings; phenomena; entities	chos rnams
contemplation	ting nge 'dzin
"creativity"	rtsal
cultivation; meditation	bsgom pa
deception; deceptive	'khrul pa
defining characteristic; by definition	mtshan nyid
energy pulse; core	snying po
entity; concreteness	dngos po
ever-fresh awareness	ye shes
"excitement"	rol pa
experience; potential for experience; mind; general forms of experience	sems
experiential sign of the development of practice	nyams
the flash of knowing that gives awareness its (illumining) quality	rig pa
(not) to be found (if inquired into)	(ma) grub pa
freedom	grol
full grasp; thorough comprehension	rtogs
fundamental alikeness	mnyam (nyid)
fundamental structuring of all experience	kun gzhi (rnam shes)
grasping of experience through thought; a thought	rtog pa
habituating tendencies	bag chags
how things appear; appearance; presence; to make itself felt	snang ba
identifiable characteristics	mtshan ma
impediment	sgrib pa

indicator; indicative	rtags
inquire into	brtag pa
limits; limiting concept; extreme	mtha'
Lord of limitations	bdud
to make really so; realize	mngon 'gyur
modes of awareness; perception	rnam shes
ongoing(ness)	ngang
open(ness); open-dimension	stong pa (nyid)
point out	bstan pa
primordial contact; dimension; communication	sku
primordial contact with the total field of events and meanings	chos sku
primordial contact with total richness and all its satisfactions	long spyod rdzogs sku
primordial experience	thugs
pure and total presence	byang chub
real meaning	nges don
relaxation	lhug pa
specific details of experience	sems 'byung
supreme, comprehensive approach	theg pa chen po
the (primordial) state of pure and total presence	byang chub sems
"symbolic encounter"	phyag rgya
that which muddies the stream of awareness	nyon mongs
there is nothing that makes (anything) what it is	bdag med
think through; think about	dpyod pa
those who are heroically committed to pure and total presence	byang chub sems dpa'
those who have come through	de bzhin gshegs pa
those who have overcome emotional conflicts	dgra bcom pa
total completeness	rdzogs chen

total field of events and meanings
ultimate content of what is
the unique fact of awareness
valid means of knowledge
ways of overcoming (limitations)

chos dbyings

chos nyid
sems nyid
tshad ma
pha rol tu phyin pa

INDEX OF TIBETAN TERMS

Printed in the United States
by Baker & Taylor Publisher Services